The cover illustration design has been created by Fred Fluker of enFocus Media Group. Previous 2009 version cover illustration was created by Emma Burns of Cranium Computing.

ISBN: 978-0-9938275-1-8

Dedication

This book is dedicated to all those amateurs like myself that search for the highest investment return but are willing to learn from someone else's mistakes. May you prosper mightily!

HIGH RISK INVESTING IS *NOT* FOR AMATEURS
Due Diligence Tips to Safeguard Your Investments

FORWARD

My mistakes, Topics to be covered, and how to use this book

How to use this book

CHAPTER 1 . . . . Pg 1
HOW *NOT* TO BUY REAL ESTATE

Downfall of Trusting; Buying a Million Dollars of Property with $70,000.00

Joint venture

Purchase Agreement

Inspections disclose problems

Refinancing is expensive

No rent verifications

Eroding cash flow

Avoiding another fiasco

Cutting the cord

Expensive lessons learned.

CHAPTER 2 . . . . Pg 14
DO I REALLY NEED TRAINING TO INVEST?

SETTING INVESTMENT GOALS

My investment plan; What kind of investor are you? Risk levels; Due diligence; Choose your focus; Financial planners; Training pointers;

My investment plan

Do I really need training to invest?

What kind of investor are you?

Money tree risk levels

What is your level of risk?

Plan your approach

Investment guidance- tax/ financial planner/broker

Don't overlook due diligence

Presentation due diligence

What are your goals?

Practical steps

    Monthly Mentor

    Success Tracs

    Pro Coach

    Billionaire Secrets to success

Start investing now

Set your investment goals

CHAPTER 3 . . . . **Pg 32**

LOW AND MODERATE RISK INVESTING

Safest; Low risk and moderate risk investments

What to invest in

Debentures, Dividends, Bonds and CDs

Safest investments

Low risk investments

Moderate risk investments

CHAPTER 4 . . . . Pg 44

EVALUATING CONDMINIUMS

Boundaries; Evaluating a condominium purchase; Reserves; Don't Let Bylaws & Policies Trip you up; New apartment Condominiums; Developer Tricks; Be Wary of Rental conversions; Bare Land Condominiums; Mixed Use Condominiums; Condominium Due Diligence List.

Condominium boundaries

Evaluating a condominium purchase

Watch out for Reserves

Don't Let Bylaws & Policies Trip you up

New apartment Condominiums

Warranties are questionable

Developer Tricks

Be Wary of Rental conversions

Bare Land Condominiums are Different

Mixed Messages In Mixed Use Condominiums

Condominium Due Diligence List.

CHAPTER 5 . . . . Pg 56

EASY TO LEARN FINANCIAL STATEMENT BASICS

Reading financial statements

Just three main reports to master

How can the same input information provide different reports?

What in heck is the accrual method?

How is money flowing in and out = cash flow statement

Don't Ignore Record Keeping

Update your Budget

Gosh is that really my Net worth?

CHAPTER 6 . . . . Pg 65
HIGH RISK INVESTING

Accredited & eligible investors; Risk Acknowledgement; Misleading sales tactics; Red flags; Investment seminars; High risk investments; Securities law; Illegal trades; Proposal documents; Can you Afford it?

Accredited & eligible investors

Risk Acknowledgement

Misleading sales tactics

Red flags

Investment seminars

High-risk investments

Securities law

Illegal trades;

Proposal documents

Can you afford it?

CHAPTER 7 . . . . Pg 80
DO YOU *REALLY* WANT TO BE A LANDLORD?

Financing my Purchase; Selling myself to a Banker; Tenants don't act like owners; Save Grief -Follow good renting procedures; Spend less on Advertising; Pets can be a Pain: Getting it Rented on my Terms; Rent verification form

Do you Really Want to be a Landlord?

Tenants don't act like Owners

Financing my purchases

Selling myself to a banker

Save grief - Follow good renting procedures

Spend less on Advertising

Pets can be a pain

Getting it rented on my terms

Rental Summary Points

NARROW ESCAPE FROM AN OLDER APARTMENT BUILDING

Narrow escape from an older apartment building

Oh Oh ! Rent controls

      Expensive lessons

      Rent Verification form

CHAPTER 8 . . . . **Pg 97**
ROOMING HOUSE HEADACHES

Upgrading the building; Purchase errors; Storage equals Revenue; Occupancy rules; Tenant Foibles; The final Straw; Tips and expensive lessons; Rental forms;

Rooming house headaches

Upgrading the building;

Purchase errors;

Storage Equals extra revenue

Occupancy rules

Tenant foibles

The final Straw

Tips & expensive lessons

Cash flow analysis

Rooming house forms

Sample rental expense

Condition report

Notice of eviction

Return of security deposit

Garage storage agreement

Security Deposit Statement

CHAPTER 9 . . . . Pg 124

MOTELS MAKE MONEY?

More mistakes and lesson tips

Motels make money?

Tips & expensive lessons

RENTAL POOLS ARE TROUBLE FREE?

Rental pools are trouble free?

The fire

Not so easy to sell

Cautions:

CHAPTER 10 . . . . Pg 141

HEADACHES OF A SIDE BY SIDE DUPLEX WITH SUITES

Illegal suites; Extra cost refinancing; Unshared maintenance expense; Unending noise & tenant Problems; Incompatible tenants; Failed Eviction; A hurried rental mistake; Derelict pickup truck; Calling it Quits; Telephone Questions; Advertising; Buying, showing & and renting tips; Rental Forms

Headaches of a side by side duplex with suites

Illegal suites

The Purchase

Extra cost refinancing

Unshared maintenance problems

Unending Noise & tenant problems

Incompatible Tenants

Skipping out

Continuing Harassment

The Failed Eviction

Non trouble free other side

A Hurried rental is a Mistake

Unpaid Utilities

Derelict pickup truck

Calling it quits: the sale

Renting tips

      Best times to advertise

      Telephone tips for prospective tenant interviews

      Showing tips

Buying tips & expensive lessons

Rental tips

Rental forms

Rental application

Acceptance of utilities & smoke detector

CHAPTER 11 . . . . Pg 166
HOW *NOT* TO INVEST IN THE STOCK MARKET
Commissions take their bite, Investment newsletters can mislead; Market moves & Trends; Forecasting methods; Master your emotions; Learn what you need to know; Learn when to sell

How not to invest in the stock market

Expensive lessons:

Various investment vehicles

Stock exchange names

Commissions take their bite

      Expensive lessons:

Investment newsletters can mislead

      Expensive lesson:

Confusing contrary market moves

      Expensive lesson

Oh Oh! Markets are seasonal

      Expensive lesson:

Market trends can be mysterious

      Expensive lesson:

Too many forecasting methods

Technical analysis chart terms can be confusing

      Expensive lesson:

Watch the change in trends

Selling too soon can be costly

Expensive lesson:

Master your emotions or you will lose

Expensive lesson:

Learn how fear & greed can forecast when to sell

Expensive lesson:

Wise investors watch industry groups

Expensive lesson:

So much information to plow through

Expensive lesson

And then there are options

Importance of fundamental analysis

CHAPTER 12 . . . . **Pg 182**

SAY NO TO PYRAMIDS

RCMP on pyramids; Investment Clubs may not be the Answer; Cautions

Say no to pyramids

Lessons learned

Investment clubs may not be your answer

Cautions:

CHAPTER 13 . . . . **Pg 193**

HIGH RISK INVESTING FOR BIG BUCKS

Risky Developments; Resorts can cheat you;

Fraudulent land development

Condominium conversion gone wrong

Cautions:

Resort Developments can cheat you

Cautions:

Sample forms

Subscription agreement

CHAPTER 14 . . . . Pg 214
OTHER OPPORTUNITIES TO CHECK INTO

Colored Diamonds Are Costly; Mortgage funds; Loan corporation bonds pay well; Other opportunities I bypassed.

Colored diamonds are costly

Expensive lesson

Mortgage investment funds pay

Cautions:

Commercial strip malls

Cautions

High interest paying developments

Cautions:

Loan corporation bonds pay

Cautions:

Other opportunities may not be all they are cracked up to be

Bank debit terminals.

U. S. Tax liens and deeds

E-bay seller

Foreclosure homes

Cautions:

AFTERWARD. . . . . Pg 226

BIBLIOGRAHY. . . . . Pg 228

BIOGRAPHY. . . . . Pg 233

DEDICATION

This book is dedicated to my eight grandchildren. May they follow their Nana's sage advice do their due diligence and receive in abundance from their own money tree investments.

FORWARD

My mistakes, the topics to be covered, and how to use this book

Good times become good memories

Bad times become great lessons

As a total amateur I made many costly mistakes If you ever wanted to know how "not" to invest, look no further.. It is described right here in the stories of my investment misadventures. This book is full of accounts from my higher risk investment mistakes, followed by pointers to help you safeguard your prized investment kitty. From real estate to pyramids schemes, colored diamonds and more, this book takes you on a journey though the pitfalls of investing. I describe the steps I took that I shouldn't have, and what steps YOU can take to prevent my failures. This book is designed to open your awareness and help protect yourself from losses. All tips and advice are designed to help you to better safeguard your investment finances.

LET ME CONGRATULATE YOU!

How wonderful! From your own regular efforts you have gathered savings to invest for your future. I applaud and congratulate you. Very few people will deny their spending desires enough to put together an investment nest egg. How fortunate you are if you also received an estate or help from a relative who also believes in you. Give yourself a well deserved pat on the back. What you have done is no small achievement.

Having acquired money to invest, you now seek investment vehicles where your money will rapidly grow. Ideally your goal is to earn at higher rates of return while your money is in safe investments. Safe investing with the banks, however, by itself will not provide the kind of gains over time that can beat inflation. You want to gain on the tax man by earning more. Investing your money in high risk ventures requires careful consideration and education before taking action.

"I always tried to turn every disaster into an opportunity"
John D. Rockefeller

"People who avoid failure also avoid success."
Robert T. Kiyosaki

MY MISTAKES

Investing in high income earning vehicles is risky, very risky! Being a single woman without a partner to review my investment plans, I am an impetuous risk taker. As such I have made costly errors that I describe in the following true stories. Unfortunately I often leapt into investments without being adequately informed. Sadly many times I gave away my hard earned dollars for nothing in return.

I was shocked at how many mistakes I have made when I wrote them all down. Do not let my errors discourage you from investing. While my stories may give you pause, don't let them dampen your enthusiasm. That is not my purpose in writing. To take pause, yes. Do more checking first, yes. Good investments are available. There are companies and projects to invest in that can make you a lot of money if you put in the right effort before you put your money down. Yes, you can become wealthy.

My mistake stories are followed by practical avoidance tips. These are presented so you can painlessly learn to prevent similar mistakes. I hope my descriptions will bring a smile or a hearty laugh if you also relate to some of these incidents.

You can make a ton of mistakes, be the biggest screwup and still survive and even succeed.

Dr. Christopher Hyatt author of *"The Psychopath's Bible"*

So many mistakes are described that you must be thinking that I am now a pauper. Not so. Even with all my losses I have amassed a comfortable living from my remaining investments. As the saying goes, if you throw enough dirt at the wall eventually some of it will stick.

As a life long learner I spent time investing in myself through reading books and attending many worthwhile training courses. These were taught by expert teachers on a cross section of investment topics. My knowledge has been gained through both good and bad experiences in many investment vehicles. Some of my experience came through buying and managing my own real estate portfolio, buying stocks on the internet, taking advice from brokers, purchasing high interest private company bonds, buying colored diamonds, investing in mortgages funds, joining an investment club and following investment newsletter guidance. I also looked into ABM machines, debit machines for taxis, vending machines, buying U.S. foreclosure properties, tax liens and start up companies.

Topics included are a variety of real estate investments, stock market investing, understanding financial statements, pyramid schemes, investment clubs, colored diamonds, resorts, frauds, and high interest paying development projects. Each article is followed by summarized pointers, provide guidance on avoiding pitfalls. Your due diligence in advance of investing will protect you, reducing costly mistakes.

HOW TO USE THIS BOOK

This book is a series of true investment failure stories. Each one contains lessons about the mistakes I made. Following each true account is a list of lessons learned and suggested cautionary tips. For heaven's sake don't repeat the same mistakes! In order to engrave the lessons in your mind I tell each account in story form to enable you to make mental pictures of the event. Your vivid mental picturing of each situation will act as mental reminders coaching you to take right action. As you recall them later, these pictures will prompt precautions when you invest. They say a picture is worth a thousand words, so make pictures as you read. They may save you money later.

While avoiding my mistakes don't forget to have a hearty laugh at my foibles.

In the first chapter I tell about my million dollar purchase attempt with resulting problems followed by the expensive lessons I learned.

CHAPTER 1

HOW *NOT* TO BUY REAL ESTATE

Trust; We attempt to buy a million dollars of property with $70,000 down

"You want to learn from experience, but you want to learn from other people's experience if you can."

Warren Buffett

In writing about my mistakes, my purpose is that I will spare you, the reader, from making similar mistakes. Before touching on basic investment planning and information in subsequent chapters here is a story of one of my costly experiences followed by tips you can use to prevent similar missteps. A number of other stories in following chapters cover a wide range of other types of my costly investment errors each followed by tips to help you to gain more and lose less.

THE DOWNFALL OF TRUSTING

My greatest weakness as an investor is that I trust people. When they say something or show me an investment plan, I trust that they are telling me the truth. I trust that when they say it is a good investment, they mean it. If they mount a great presentation I trust what it says. If they say they are experts I believe them. Oh boy did my trust get me into trouble! I trusted so much that I did little checking into either the presenter's background or the deal. I saw only the dollars I would make. I was a high risk investor.

BUYING A MILLION DOLLARS WORTH OF PROPERTY

"Rich people focus on opportunities. Poor people focus on obstacles."

T. Harv Eker

Being a novice at purchasing a package of real estate with low money down provided an intense learning curve. We were so inexperienced! There is a saying "buyers are liars" but vendors can also be liars, I found out to my sorrow.

Amusingly, however, the situation also won my lady friend and me trophies from Raymond Aaron, a real estate guru and coach, for being the "Players of the Year." He told envious meeting attendees that we had bought a million dollars worth of property for $70,000 down. None of them knew that the deal had already collapsed.

My friend, (I'll call her Ann to protect her privacy), and I enrolled in Raymond Aaron's Monthly Mentor course. We thought it was going to teach us how to buy real estate, but its focus was goal setting. However, encouraged by networking with others members we connected with Paul a member of the Real Estate Investment Network (R.E.I.N). Paul (not his real name) told us he had a lead on 7 pieces of property worth at least a million dollars that could be purchased with only $70,000.00 down. He was looking for partners with money. We knew nothing about Paul but he seemed self assured and sounded experienced.

STARTING THE JOINT VENTURE

"Often in the real world, it's not the smart that get ahead

but the bold."

Robert T .Kiyosaki

Meeting Paul and his friend in a coffee shop we decided to form a joint venture to purchase these properties. We knew nothing about Paul's background but he sounded knowledgeable. Paul would be the real estate finding partner, his friend the carpenter to make repairs and Ann and I would provide funds. We would all be equal partners.

Tailoring a R.E.I.N joint venture agreement to suit our circumstances, Paul took it to a real estate lawyer. The lawyer recommended that we incorporate a company to hold the properties instead of writing a joint venture agreement.

With the vendor's addresses in hand we drove around to see the exteriors of the properties that Paul introduced us to. They were a 10 suiter building, two side by side duplexes, a condominium apartment, a half duplex and two houses, one with a basement suite.

The vendor met us and first showed us through the newly painted vacant main floor suite of a nice looking well located up/down house. He said it had already been rented for $850 a month plus utilities. The basement suite was currently rented for $450.00 to a lady with several cats. The vendor said she had been given a rent increase to $500.00. It turned out that this house was the nicest of the whole batch. It certainly whetted our interest.

SIGNING THE PURCHASE AGREEMENT

We signed a conditional purchase agreement in December for $993,000.00 including vendor take back mortgages on most houses totaling $189,920.00. We wrote in conditions of mortgage assumptions, inspections and verification of rents. The vendor provided information about mortgage balances and payments on the properties saying that all mortgages were assumable. Our lawyer advised in writing that legal fees for this deal would be $5,000.00 plus $2,200.00 of disbursements.

Setting possession for February 1st, we began inspecting interiors. Taking on the financial partner role, I made spread sheets; constantly updating income projections, I had also anticipated repair expense, and estimates of our likely return.

Information provided on the ten suite building indicated a 9.9% cap rate if rents were increased by $25.00 per unit. The numbers looked like we would have good positive cash flow of about $14,000.00 a year after allowing for normal repairs, a 5% vacancy and several small rent increases. We were excited!

Pretty soon it became apparent that Paul's carpenter friend was not contributing.
We dropped him out leaving three of us to complete our company incorporation. For our protection Ann and I held 51% of the voting shares between us since we were the only ones with anything to lose. We each placed $40,000.00 in the corporate bank account for the $70,000.00 down payment, plus legal and other expenses. Neither of us had additional funds that we could easily contribute.

INSPECTIONS DISCLOSE PROBLEMS

Then problems reined down on us. Initial inspections of the older apartment building disclosed many needed repairs: carpets to replace; painting to do; and suspect boiler leaks.

Regardless of attempts to persuade him otherwise the second mortgage lender on the building would not let us assume his mortgage. He would have to be paid out. That meant refinancing.

REFINANCING IS EXPENSIVE

We made an application to a trust company, the current lender, requesting a new mortgage to include $30,000.00 or more for required repairs. Following their inspector's on site review they required us to obtain a number of reports before they would render their lending decision. They requested a value appraisal, engineer's reports on roof and boiler systems, and an insurance appraisal. We would also be required to pay to the trust company a 0.5% fee based on mortgage value for their review. We grudgingly accepted, ordering the reports, but expenses were now beginning to badly erode our reduced reserve fund.

While our purchase price for that building was $300,000.00 the appraisal came back at only $285,000.00. So we negotiated an amendment with the vendor to reduce our contract price by $15,000.00.

My next inspection disclosed several problem tenants that were living in the two run down side by side duplexes. Renovations needed were; paint, replacement of damaged flooring and rotted fences. Several appliance and roof replacements also loomed on the horizon. The vendor said that rent increases had been given out. Up to $750.00 a month each from the $650.00 the tenants told me they were presently paying.

Then we discovered that the vendor did not even have title to the duplexes! He was not even the owner! His father was. The vendor assured us that his father had agreed to sell.

When the trust company's mortgage approval was finally received on the 10 suiter, we negotiated a $5,000.00 discount for cash payout of the second mortgage. That would provide us extra funds to offset our rising costs. However the trust company's mortgage approval letter added further inspection requirements. These were to be obtained from Emergency Response Department, Building Inspection, utility provider, and an Environmental Law Centre search. It appeared our small payout gain would also be eaten up. Our hearts fell when we discovered we would have to update the fire system to install wired-in heat detectors in every suite. We were relieved when we were able to make a deal with the vendor to cover this expense.

A number of apartment suites and one house was still un-inspected. Looking at that older house on the outside it had water stains on its soffits and stucco walls that to me looked problematic. The stains could be indicating roof and interior damage caused by ice damming, and the potential for mould to start inside the walls.

Time was moving on but our initial requests for information, rent verifications and full building proforma had still not been provided.

Since I was about to embark on a preplanned five week trip to India in early January, Ann and Paul took over. Our lawyers had not received information or adjustments from the vendor's lawyer so they advised Paul and Ann to extend possession date. It was extended to March 1st.

NO RENT VERIFICATIONS

On my return in mid February I found out that Paul had cursorily inspected the other properties, without making repair lists. To my horror I learned he had also signed off all conditions without ever having received rent verifications or an actual expense proforma!

Nor had the vendor's lawyer prepared any of the adjustments yet! Backing out of the deal at this point would mean deposit forfeiture but it was beginning to look like the necessary repairs could bankrupt us in the process.

Telling Raymond Aaron at a meeting in February about our purchase I asked about not having received rent verifications. He replied

"There is no reason a vendor would not provide this information unless he has something to hide."

Now I was doubly concerned.

ENDLESS DELAYS - ERODING CASH FLOW

"Wealth measures how much money your money is making
and therefore, your financial survivability."

Robert T .Kiyosaki

On March 1st we finally received a very simple building proforma. It did not include caretaking or grounds keeping at all, and indicated different revenue and expense than we had been told. I was very upset. The other partners were relying on my numbers but with all the extra costs added there was no longer any cash flow left in my projections. It was becoming very dicey. Paul "poo pooed" my concerns saying it was still such a great deal. Of course he had nothing to lose; only Ann and I were at risk.

Our lawyer seemed to be sending out a number of uninitiated letters to us which we asked him to cease. We felt he was just trying to make himself more money. Days passed. Still no information from the vendor's lawyer, so possession was moved once again first to a date in April and then to May 1st.

In desperation our lawyer's staff began to prepare the time consuming adjustments with information I submitted. May 1st passed by, and still no verifications were forthcoming. Finally our lawyers arranged a face to face meeting in mid May to see if the deal could be saved.

In a heightened state of anxiety Ann and I went to the lawyer's office. Facing the vendor and his lawyer across the board room table we finally learned the truth. The vendor had to disclose that there were actually a number of vacancies, including the unrented main floor of the first house we were shown five months before. Then the vendor sheepishly admitted that rent increases had not been given to any tenants after all. We were thoroughly annoyed to have been deliberately cheated. Perhaps the vendor had seen us as easy marks for his cheating scheme. Our spirits deflated. Any last possibility to make the sale work disappeared at that table.

The vendor's failure to provide information requested in the purchase agreement gave us the opportunity to walk away from the sale without forfeiture of our deposit. Our lawyer suggested that a law suit for damages would be expensive so that idea was dropped.

We learned later that the vendor's lawyer was notorious for his practice of pushing adjustment preparation onto a purchaser's lawyer to save his client money.

We were shocked to be presented with a bill for $11,357.00 in legal fees. They included charges for unnecessary correspondence work we had earlier chided our lawyer about. We finally settled the total bill for $8,000.00 with the senior partner.

Three months after our settlement was paid we were surprised to receive a letter from our lawyer. It said that two other legal bills were still outstanding for mortgage transfer work by other lawyers. No way were we going to pay the lawyer any more money. In light of our total settlement we refused payment and our lawyer ultimately had to settle with the other firms.

AVOIDING ANOTHER FIASCO

After this sale collapsed Paul found another property to purchase. An old three story combined commercial and apartment building in a strip mall style. We looked at it from the outside and completed another conditional offer.

My inspection of this building again yielded expensive potential problems. An unfinished part of the basement with cracked concrete and soil floors showed signs of past water problems. The two floors of suites above the offices were in need of painting, carpets and some renovation but were livable and occupied. The parking lot at the rear of the building was in need of patching.

We discovered that the commercial area tenant was a government department whose five year lease was about to expire. Being the only commercial tenant their possible move out could leave both the main and basement levels vacant, a loss of over 60% of the revenue. That was likely the vendor's motivation to sell.

We didn't need any further inspections to tell us to drop it and wisely walked away from this money pit "opportunity" also, with no loss of money.

CUTTING THE CORD

"You can't make a good deal with a bad person."

Warren Buffett

We then asked Paul to give up his interest in our corporation to which he agreed. His ideas of good deals certainly did not mesh with ours. In the meantime we had learned more about him. We realized he was too greedy and entrepreneurial with no regard for details or follow up. We had been naïve innocents caught up by our inexperience.

Ann and I paid dearly for these lessons. Our out of pocket expenses were close to $13,000.00.

EXPENSIVE LESSONS LEARNED

1. When taking on a partner do thorough due diligence into the person's background and references before agreeing to anything. Do not presume the person is an expert.

2. Talk to a lawyer to determine and set up the method by which you will become partners.

3. Obtain titles to all properties before or as soon as you make your conditional offer.

4. Verify with the lenders on title all amounts due and whether all mortgages or second mortgages may be assumable.

5. Do not trust a vendor's verbal rent statements. Get proof.

6. Request copies and review actual rental lease agreements for length and terms.

7. Obtain written, signed verifications of rents and utilities from each tenant. When tenant signed verification of rents are not forthcoming in a reasonable time the vendor may have something to hide.

8. Prepare a spreadsheet to list anticipated expenses and revenue, updating it as new information becomes available.

9. Obtain an insurance quotation to build the numbers into your spreadsheet.

10. Limit exposure to expensive lawyer's fees by doing as much ground work as you can.

11. Do you have enough contingency funds to proceed? Costs could be considerably greater than you expect.

12. Conduct thorough inspections with written repair lists and obtain repair quotations to eliminate surprises prior to being

committed to the purchase. Hire an inspection firm to review the property if you have any doubts at all.

13. Watch for any signs of water problems. Telltale signs of roof ice damming are stains on the siding below the overhanging soffit. Ice damming occurs when freeze thaw cycles gradually build up ice along the roof eaves. The ice expands up the roof pushing under the shingles. The roof eaves are normally protected with a starter course of plastic or tar paper on older homes that does not extend very far up the roof from the edge. When the weather turns warm enough the ice begins to melt and water drips through the soffits and often into the house interior. Moist materials like drywall ceilings and wood framed walls are perfect hosts for the growth of mould.

    Water in the basement that has seeped in will leave mineral evidence along the joint between floor and wall or along the pathways of flow.

14. Placing a new mortgage on an old building can be expensive and time consuming. There may be requests for required appraisals, environmental assessment, fire, boiler, roof and other inspections, mortgage placement fees, legal fees, etc. Plus there is the likelihood of having to meet current building and fire codes.

15. Verify through inspections whether older properties require expensive repairs.

16. Obtain thorough background and credit checks of tenants with signed lease agreements or you may inherit potential problems trying to collect the rent.

17. Make certain that condition reports were prepared with the tenants when they moved in. You will need these for damage

verification when tenants move out or you will have to pay yourself for any damage restoration expense.

18. Get assistance from a mentor if tackling something unfamiliar.

19. In addition when you make a purchase offer:

- Be sure you list all of your conditions and terms to be provided by the vendor in your offer to purchase.

- Allow yourself more time than you think may be necessary to obtain the required information or to remove the conditions when buying a commercial property.

- If financing is to be obtained allow sufficient time to obtain mortgage approval. A commercial property or an apartment building will require considerably more time to remortgage than a residential purchase. It may take several months time because of the required inspections and reports.

- Let your lawyer review your agreement before it is presented to the vendor or make one of your conditions a legal review.

20. Don't be afraid to challenge your lawyer's fees if necessary.

AND LASTLY IF A DEAL SOUNDS TOO GOOD TO BE TRUE, IT LIKELY IS!

A sample spreadsheet for tracking a multiple purchase investment follows.

PROPERTY ANALYSIS

MORTGAGES

Addresses	First Mortgage	Second Mortgage	Third Mortgage	Cash Down	Total Price	2nd Mortge Amortization	Interest Rate 2nd	Term End 1st Mortgage
1	$ 79,750.31	$ 21,749.69	$ -	$ 8,500.00	$ 110,000.00	25	7.31555	date
2	$ 59,690.37	$ 25,366.64	$ -	$ 9,922.99	$ 95,000.00	25	7.31555	date
3	$ 94,770.19	$ 30,672.44	$ -	$ 11,557.37	$ 137,000.00	25	7.31555	date
4	$ 93,287.48	$ 30,675.38	$ -	$ 11,037.14	$ 135,000.00	25	7.31555	date
5	$ 56,022.84	$ 8,977.16	$ -	$ -	$ 65,000.00	25	7.31555	date
6	$ 83,554.66	$ 24,962.84	$ -	$ 16,482.50	$ 125,000.00	25	7.31555	date
$ 467,075.85	$ 142,424.15	$ -	$ 57,500.00	$ 667,000.00				

MONTHLY PAYMENTS

Addresses	Payment 1st Mortge	Payment 2nd Mortge	Payment 3rd Mortge	Insurance	Property Tax (Condo)	Total Payments	Monthly Rent	Security Deposit	Cash Flow
1	$ 671.00	$ 159.11	$ -	20.92		$ 851.03	$ 650.00	$ -	(201.03)
2	$ 512.81	$ 185.72	$ -	20.92		$ 719.46	$ 800.00	$ 500.00	80.55
3	$ 636.63	$ 224.39	$ -	19.25	$ 156.82	$ 1,037.09	$ 750.00	$ 750.00	(287.09)
4	$ 627.75	$ 224.41	$ -	19.25	$ 155.58	$ 1,027.00	$ 650.00	$ -	(377.00)
5	$ 519.00	$ 65.67	$ -		$ 158.51	$ 743.18	$ 650.00	$ 500.00	(93.18)
6	$ 921.95	$ 182.62	$ -	20.08		$ 1,124.65	$ 850.00	$ -	(274.65)
6 suite							$ 450.00	$ -	450.00
Total	$ 3,889.15	$ 1,041.91	$ -	100.42	470.91	$ 5,502.39	$ 4,900.00	$ 1,750.00	(702.39)

Proposed Rent Increase	$ 100.00	$ (196.00)
Less 4% vacancy	$ (196.00)	$ (196.00)
	$ 4,704.00	$ (698.39)
	$ 4,900.00	$ (702.39)

TOTAL ANNUAL PAYMENTS	$ 58,800.00	$ 56,448.00	ANNUAL LOSS	$ (10,780.69)

13

CHAPTER 2

DO I REALLY NEED TRAINING TO INVEST ?

My investment plan; What kind of investor are you? Risk levels;
Due diligence; Choose your focus; Financial planners; Safest
investments; Training pointers;

*"When you know you are ignorant in a subject, start
educating yourself by finding an expert in the field or find
a book on the subject."*

Robert T .Kiyosaki

MY INVESTMENT PLAN

In previous years I had been a Realtor selling both new homes for
builders as well as general real estate. Twenty-five years ago I left that
sales area to become a property manager focusing on condominium
management. When Ron LeGrande taught a real estate course about
different ownership options, I decided on a real estate acquisition
plan. Ron's ownership options were buying, renovating and flipping;
buying to sell wholesale; buying to hold; and buying to sell lease
options. As a single woman without a handyman bone in my body
my choice was to buy and hold real estate.

My loosely developed investment plan was to build up a portfolio of
real estate properties. Then as I neared retirement I would sell one
property a year to invest the money in other vehicles. At the age of
58, I used the proceeds from the sale of my management business to
buy my first property, a half duplex. As its value increased I
refinanced, taking out the equity to buy an up/down duplex near the
university. Eventually I had title to eleven properties, including
condominium units, half duplexes, a rooming house and a small
interest in a land parcel. Then in my mid sixties on the advice of my
tax accountant I began to sell one property a year in order not to
have to pay all my gains to the government.

Once I began to divest myself of real estate I started to invest in a variety of vehicles, such as mortgage funds, development bonds, construction mortgage financing, financial bonds, stocks, etc. I did not put all of my eggs in one basket so to speak. If one investment turned bad and I lost everything, I would still have other avenues earning income for me. With stock investments (after I learned my lessons the hard way) I selected one commodity industry, uranium, to focus on. I spread my risk by owning shares in several companies within that industry.

I am what the analysts would call a "hot" person. I am a high risk taker. I tend to grab at opportunities without thorough research first. Being a high risk type has certainly cost me many lost dollars over the years. In my "how not to" stories that follow I tell you about my failures, but also give you tips on how to avoid making the same mistakes.

First let's look at some basic understandings.

DO I REALLY NEED TRAINING TO INVEST?

How much money do you want to lose from unwise investments? You wouldn't think of becoming a plumber or a hair dresser without getting training first, would you? Do you relate getting trained to investing safely? I didn't at first but I certainly do now. I bet I have lost one hundred fifty thousand dollars in all through not doing my due diligence before investing.

Training is available on line from many great sources. A variety of worthwhile courses as well as investment conferences are available. A list of courses and helpful books is provided in the bibliography. T. Harv Eker, of Peak Potentials Training puts on a Millionaire School where you can be introduced to ideas for investment as well as training opportunities. Investfest, put on by the Freedom Investment Club each year, provides four jam packed days of top level training with an array of investment opportunities. This is where I met Bill

Bartmann, Brian Tracey, investment brokers, business coaches and other great trainers.

Many books and other training tools are available once you select your area of investment interest. Seek out groups that are teaching that specialty and join them. You will meet and network with some really helpful people. Yes it will cost money, but in the end it will return many dollars in benefits.

If you wish to learn about where to invest Jordan E. Goodman's book *"Everyone's Money Book On Retirement Planning"* covers all investment areas and planning for retirement. It is helpful to gain basic understanding of investment vehicles and risk planning. Jordan includes many lists of helpful resources as well as American tax planning strategies.

Learning how to read and make sense of financial statements is a must. Financial statement basics are covered later in this chapter. I found Robert Kiyosaki's video on financial statements was very helpful for a start. Also Keith Cunningham's Keys to the Vault course, where he takes you through the financial statements of the Lemon Aid Company. Suze Orman's book *"Women & Money"* is to the point. Once you have a basic understanding you cannot find a better financial statement training guide than *"Warren Buffett and the Interpretation of Financial Statements"* by Mary Buffett and David Clark.

Excellent courses taught by professional coaches can really assist you to not only set your goals, but to meet and exceed them over time. I found it difficult to set goals until I took the Success Tracs course offered by Peak Potential Training from Andrew Barber Starkey. He now offers his professional services through Procoach.com, and has helped many people to exceed their goals. Raymond Aaron taught his Monthly Mentor program to help me set better goals and gain investing understanding. Many books on goal setting are also available through new and used book stores and on line through Amazon.

One of the very best books I discovered for setting achievement goals was Bill Bartmann's book titled *"Billionaire Secrets to Success"*. Not only did it turn my goals into promises but it bolstered my self esteem. It got me totally fired up and performing to reach my goals. It included questions that really changed my way of relating to success. Bill also has a complete course with DVDs and CDs as well as a separate workbook that includes the *"Billionaire Secrets of Success"* book. It was too bad that I came upon it so late in life. Bill has a recent book, *"Bail out Riches, How Everyday Investors can Make a Fortune Buying Bad Loans for Pennies on the Dollar"* in which he teaches you how you can copy his method to turn collecting bad debt into a good income.

I joined Peak Potentials Training and attended a number of T. Harv Eker's courses, giving me the courage to step out on my own. Each day as I drove to work I listened to training tapes and CD's on a variety of self development and investment topics. Peak Potential's Millionaire School audio sets with each tape introducing a new trainer or investment contact was very instructional.

I also attended real estate and landlording programs put on by Wright Thurston, Tim Johnson and Don Campbell of the Real Estate Investment Network (R.E.I.N). This provided excellent training while I enjoyed my membership. Their Quick Start program taught the basics of how to make money with little money down through real estate investing. Ron LeGrande taught four methods of real estate investing. Ozzie Jurrock, Albert Lawry and Robert Allen were also among my teachers.

I began to gradually understand more about the real estate investment business. I obtained and read copies of the Residential Tenancies Act. I learned about my rights and those of my tenants. In my previous career as a Realtor I had learned about contract law and how to prepare contracts. This was an invaluable tool.

Robert Allen's *"No Money Down"* and various other real estate books and courses can get you off to a good start toward your real estate goals. Although the real estate market has taken a deep dive in the US and parts of Canada due to the sub prime lending fiasco, people will always require housing. While prices are down there are opportunities to buy that can provide cash flow again due to the lowered prices. Study the market thoroughly before entering.

The Freedom Investment Club course *7 Keys to Financial Enlightenment* is an excellent home study course covering understanding yourself and knowing your goals, developing your financial plan, investing in a business, successful investing, building you financial team and staying motivated.

There are many ways to find good investments. People are happy to tell you of their successes mechanisms that you can then look into. Networking groups can lead you to good vehicles to place your money in. One such group is CEO Space. They hold regular networking meetings in various cities. Often investment firms seeking capital advertise in the business section of your local newspaper. They will be grateful to send you information. There may be presentation meetings to attend as well.

WHAT KIND OF INVESTOR ARE YOU?

Your personality affects your investing type. It is important to your levels of tolerable personal stress to stay within your comfort zone. Your values, how you relate to money and your understanding of finance will all affect the type of investing you want to take part in. For instance, a more analytical person with discipline and focus may not want to invest in the high flyers. They would prefer the more stable steady opportunities.

Your age also needs to be taken into consideration. When you are in your twenties and thirties you may want to take on more risk than when you are nearing retirement. As you are nearing retirement your need for regular receipts from your investments and the safety of your investments may be paramount in your planning. Financial planners recommend establishing a risk tolerance portfolio based on your age and your future needs and goals. It will include a percentage of your investment in each of the four categories: High risk, moderate risk, low risk and the safest levels.

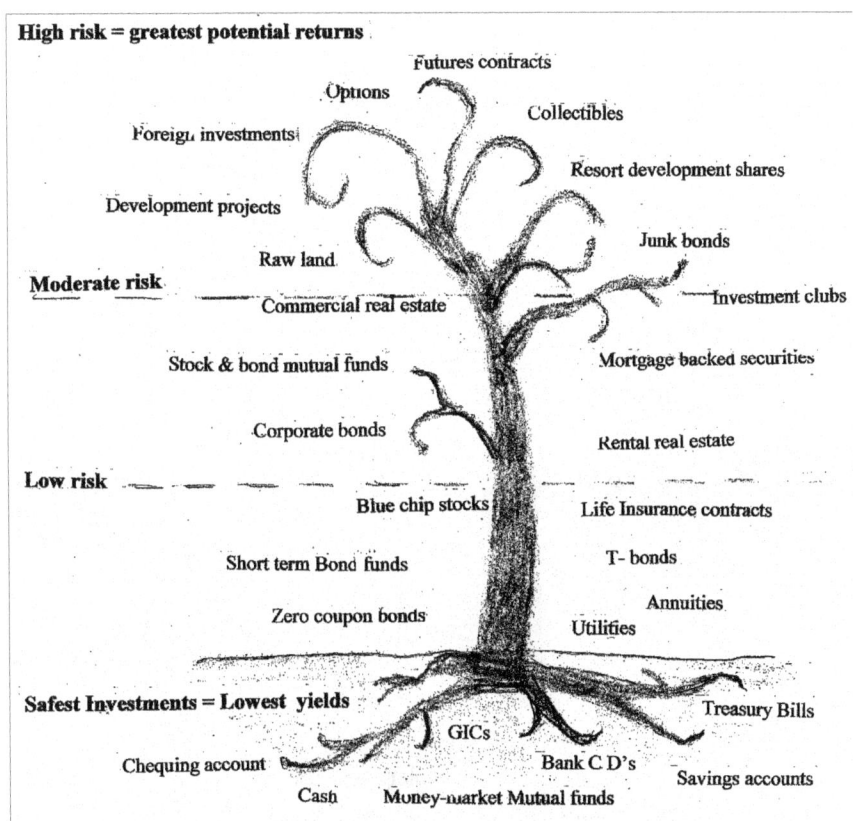

High risk = greatest potential returns

Futures contracts

Options

Collectibles

Foreign investments

Resort development shares

Development projects

Junk bonds

Raw land

Moderate risk

Commercial real estate

Investment clubs

Stock & bond mutual funds

Mortgage backed securities

Corporate bonds

Rental real estate

Low risk

Blue chip stocks

Life Insurance contracts

Short term Bond funds

T- bonds

Zero coupon bonds

Annuities

Utilities

Safest Investments = Lowest yields

Treasury Bills

GICs

Chequing account

Bank C D's

Savings accounts

Cash

Money-market Mutual funds

MONEY TREE RISK LEVELS

WHAT IS YOUR LEVEL OF RISK?

Before you put out your first investment dollar it is really important to know yourself and your comfort level. Then stick within it if you want to sleep at night. It will spare you a great deal of worry and stress to invest in the right vehicles for your comfort zone. Things to consider are your risk tolerance, your net worth, and your retirement plans.

1. How many months or years do have available to invest before you require the funds?

2. Are you conservative? Is safety of your investment a major concern?

3. Are you cautious but not too conservative?

4. Are you a risk taker? Are you into aggressive investing? Are you willing to gamble looking for superior capital appreciation? You may lose a lot more than a more conservative investor.

5. How comfortable are you with potential short term losses? Sometimes you may experience losses in the short run that can be large gains if held long enough.

6. How comfortable are you with losses for longer terms of a year or more that may still indicate potential gains down the road?

7. What is your overall tolerance for risk? Can you create a formula that you will be comfortable with?

8. Consider that while more risk means more potential gains there is no guarantee that you will actually make higher gains.

9. Remember no investment is risk free.

10. You are on your own. Do not count on the Securities Commission or government to vet and protect every investment opportunity.

PLAN YOUR APPROACH

"If you have little money and you want to be rich, you must first be "focused" not "balanced."

Robert T .Kiyosaki

Evaluate your current financial situation, and then where you want to be financially. Create an investment formula using percentages that sets a percentage limit of investment in each area. This can include some high income potential as well as safer low income guaranteed earnings. For example if you are a low risk personality you may want to put 50% of your investment dollars into safe or low risk investments, perhaps 40% into moderate risk investments and only 10% into high risk investments. This type of investment plan can give you the best of both protection and possible growth.

If you are starting later in life, like I did, you may want to structure a formula with less in the low risk category, say 30% and more in the high risk category, perhaps 30%, with 40% in moderate risk. If you are uncertain what plan to create, seek assistance. During the current downturn those that invested in balanced portfolios that included half of their investment in bonds saw a much lower percentage of loss in value over the last year when compared to stocks and equity funds.

If you start your investment plan while in your twenties you have a distinct advantage over someone who begins investing in their forties or fifties. If you are planning for future retirement there is a need to earn more than inflation if possible. Inflation and taxes will both impact your investment plan. Be mindful that living costs escalate over the years based on the rate of inflation. At a 4% rate of inflation your living costs will be more than double in twenty years time. At an 8% inflation rate they will be close to five times higher than they are at present.

INVESTMENT GUIDANCE –TAX/ FINANCIAL PLANNER/ BROKER

"Most brokers are not created equal. Find a broker who has your best interests at heart."

Robert T .Kiyosaki

You may find it of value to discuss your plans with a tax specialist, broker or financial planner who can help you to devise an investing plan. When you begin your investment plan both inflation and tax avoidance measures need to be taken into consideration. This is where professional advice can effectively provide guidance.

If you have a large sum to invest it is best to get the advice of your tax specialist as well as an investment broker or financial planner before making any commitments.

A tax specialist can help you save tax and direct you to investments that earn more after tax considerations are taken into account. I was very grateful to receive the advice I did. During my portfolio buildup the specialist helped me save on current tax. When I came to sell my real estate holdings through her guidance I was able to preserve more of my capital gain.

A financial planner may charge an hourly or specific rate to review and set up a plan for you and provide ongoing advice. A knowledgeable planner can make suggestions to tailor your plan to your specific financial tolerance levels and situation.

Most brokers earn their living through making commissions on the stocks or investment opportunities they sell. You will not directly pay for your broker's advice but will be charged a commission on what ever stock you may purchase or sell through the broker. Be clear about what the fees will be. I was shocked to have my purchase and sales commissions go from $95.00 a trade to over $165.00 a trade without my realization. Since I was purchasing small share lots my shares had to gain a great deal just to break even. I soon changed to an online brokerage instead, at $25.00 a trade. Others comfortable with internet brokers will pay even less per trade, some as low as $3.00 each.

Your broker may get paid through generating trading activity. If trading is left up to that type of broker you may find a lot of unwarranted activity occurs on your account. Be mindful that brokers also get commissions from the company whose initial public offering (IPO) or other offering they are trying to sell. Be aware of this and do your own checking into whether the offering is really viable for you. The broker's enthusiasm can be misleading. Be mindful when you take their advice.

Find out what they specialize in. Some will specialize in certain market areas like small cap corporation start-ups (IPOs). Others may specialize in commodity groups, etc.

When you select a broker, don't let him or her forget about you. You want them to constantly keep your account in mind to provide you advice as market conditions change. I recommend that you keep in constant weekly or biweekly contact with your broker. You must also regularly review your statements and question the broker about anything you don't understand.

Review your investing strategy with your broker. A simple investment strategy is best for a beginner.

Exercise care in your selection of a financial planner or broker. Interview them about themselves and their business;

- Is the individual or firm registered?
- What are their credentials?
- Are they in good standing with the securities commission?
- Check your securities commission for any investigations or reporting complaints.
- How do they make their money?
- What do they specialize in? Does it fit your goals?
- How well do they look after their clients?
- How much have they earned for their clients?
- Have their recommendations kept up or surpassed the inflation rate?
- What are their fees or commission rates?
- Ask whether there are any other fees or charges.
- How easily are you able to contact him or her?
- What kind of reporting do they provide and how often?

Inclusive financial planning that encompasses your home mortgage, life insurance plus a personally tailored investment plan are also available. You may find a combination plan to be beneficial for your family. One such networking firm that offers inclusive combination plans is Primerica Financial Services. Several of my grandchildren have got off to great starts toward building their wealth using the Primerica system.

DON'T OVERLOOK DUE DILIGENCE. *DUE DILIGENCE IS CRITICAL!*

"I would venture to say that it is the lack of personal self discipline that is the No. 1 delineating factor between the rich, the poor and the middle class."

Robert T .Kiyosaki

DUE DILIGENCE IS CRITICAL TO INVESTMENT SUCCESS

When I started investing, I did not do enough back ground checking. Is it any wonder I lost money? It is the main key to successful investing. Checking all aspects of the proposed investment before putting your money down is absolutely necessary. One poorly placed investment can cripple you financially. What is adequate due diligence? If you are uncertain to what extent you need to check into an investment before placing your money on the line, the Freedom Investment Club has an excellent course on *The Art of Due Diligence* written by John Tansowny.

John Tansowny's definition of due diligence:

"The systematic evaluation of an opportunity using some fundamental tools and asking some fundamental questions to be certain you have information and data in front of you to make a sound "go/no go" investment decision."

In order to perform due diligence on a company here are some questions to answer:

25

1. Do the management people have integrity?

2. Is the company registered with the securities regulator?

3. Is the company private or public?

4. How many years have they been in business?

5. How knowledgeable are they in their field?

6. What educational or professional training do the principals have?

7. How are the principals and employees paid? Is it by salary, commissions or specified fees?

8. What do you know about the product?

9. Is there or will there be a market for the product?

10. How competitive is their product in the market?

11. How healthy or profitable is the company?

12. What is the corporate structure? How are they organized?

13. Are there any unpaid obligations for taxes or legal claims?

14. Is there a business plan in place? Can you receive a copy?

15. Can you receive client references?

16. What funding is being sought or is required?

17. Will they hold a competent corporate presentation?

18. Is there a lock in period?

19. Can you resell your purchase to another?

20. How can you get your money back?

21. What is your exit strategy? Does it fit your time line?

22. What written information is available?

a)   Prospectus or offering memorandum

b)   Annual financial report

c)   Quarterly or interim statements

d)   News release

e)   Risk statements

PRESENTATION DUE DILIGENCE

1.   If the promoter puts on a demonstration how professional is it?

2.   Is there any pressure to sign up right now? Spur of the moment hype and pressure may lead to a bad decision on your part.

3.   Do they allow a cooling off period, perhaps 72 hours, where you can change your mind and get your deposit back?

4.   Can you take the papers away with you to review before signing?

To gain more and lose less, no matter what you decide to invest in, do your due diligence first. Give yourself peace of mind by completing a due diligence check list on the person and or company. Then make an informed decision. If there is one thing you take away from this book I hope it is recognition of the importance of completing due diligence *before* investing.

WHAT ARE YOUR GOALS?

Some of the very best training I received was learning how to set goals. I had trouble with goal setting. I knew I had a general direction I wanted to go in but never had the steps or a plan set up. I had kind of drifted through life, and I didn't really know what I wanted for far too many years. Now I know that if I want to achieve anything I must first put the thought out there. I must have an intention toward something. I must write it down and measure my progress toward it regularly. Then I must take small steps toward its achievement.

What would you like to achieve? I have found that unless I have distinct ideas about what I want I achieve little.

PRACTICAL STEPS

There are many goal setting books and courses available today. While they teach similar skills you may want to select a method to follow that will work for you. Several are described below.

Monthly mentor

Raymond Aaron's "Monthly Mentor" is a worthwhile course on goal setting, with monthly meetings. Raymond's motto is "Double your income doing something you love." His detailed workbook system includes the aspects of cleaning up messes, acknowledgment, increasing wealth, trying and learning something new, and doing something for yourself. His plan includes working backwards from the final goal achievement to the present moment, while listing the steps needed to achieve the goals. Raymond Aaron can be contacted through his web site www.monthlymentor.com.

Success Tracs coaching program

Success Tracs put on by Peak Potentials Training Systems also holds regular meetings. They provide guidance and detailed workbooks to track your progress. Each week there are weekly and quarterly intentions to set. In addition there is always an opportunity to work with a success partner to help keep focused between sessions. Networking time is also set aside each meeting. While you might not notice a lot of improvement in the first year while using the system, by the third year you should really begin to see great results.

Pro Coach System

Andrew Barber Starkey used to teach Success Tracs and then began his own coaching and goal setting course under the name of ProCoach. My friends that attend are making very successful progress. You may contact him through his web site www.procoachsystem.com

Billionaire Secrets to Success

Goal setting had always been difficult for me until I finally connected with Bill Bartmann's book and course called *"Billionaire Secrets to Success"* His goal suggestions are so succinct and simple. Bill's workbook is different from those in other goal setting courses. He approaches goal setting by building up your self esteem and gets you to make your promise plan and list of notable achievements. As Bill suggested I may not meet my goals but I always keep my promises. Working through his suggestions really got me activated.

START INVESTING NOW

"The habit of managing your money is more important than the amount."

T. Harv Eker

Don't put it off. Starting my investment program so late in life, at age 58, I felt I no longer had time to let my investment dollars build slowly and safely. I went right into moderate and high risk investments only. Not the safest plan. Yes, it has cost me but it also pushed me up the financial gain ladder.

It's best to start your investment program in your twenties if you can. At that age even small amounts religiously set aside each month can grow into fortunes by retirement time. Many families with growing children are so focused on putting education money away but overlook their own looming retirement needs. Many single women do not want to face the reality of reaching retirement without investment income to augment meager social security or Canada pension plans. If they don't take money each month to begin to build a retirement nest egg, they face moving into a friend's back bedroom in order to survive. You may not think you have money to invest, but you have options on how you spend the money you do have. Look at what you want, what you need and what you have and devise your plan. Why not rearrange your spending to set aside some of your money to invest for the future.

Design and follow an investment plan or get help to create one from a financial planner. After you devise your investment plan you will want to become familiar with the investment opportunities available and the ways in which you earn money from each.

SET YOUR INVESTMENT GOALS

Before starting to invest, set your goals. What do you need from investing? Have you any idea of your current net worth? A good place to start is to list your assets and liabilities to see your financial starting point.

1. What do you want to achieve and by when?
   a) Are you trying to keep pace with inflation and possibly outperform inflation?

   b) Are you wanting to produce regular income?

c) Are you looking for a combination of income as well as capital
appreciation over time?

d) Are you focused on getting capital appreciation without needing income at this time?

2. How will you spread your risk?

3. How long do you plan to accumulate and hold real estate or higher risk investments?

4. What is your exit plan?

5. Then what? What will you then invest in?

6. Where will you get the money to invest?

In the following chapter I review low and moderate risk investments.

CHAPTER 3

LOW AND MODERATE RISK INVESTING

Safest Investments; Low risk and moderate risk investments

Listed in this chapter are short descriptions for types of investments. More detailed considerations are described for specific types of investment in following chapters.

Unfortunately due to the recent world wide recession brought on by over leveraging of investments, even some "safe" investment vehicles may no longer be as safe as they were considered to be.

WHAT TO INVEST IN

"You must know the difference between an asset and a liability, and buy assets. If you want to be rich, this is all you need to know."

Robert T. Kiyosaki

There are real tangible assets such as real estate, commodities, gold, silver, platinum or palladium, etc. Then there are financial paper assets such as mortgages, certificates of deposit (CDs or GICs), bonds, stock certificates in public companies, private company shares or bonds, debentures, mutual funds and investment trusts as well as foreign exchange cash. Each type of asset has many variations.

DEBENTURES, DIVIDENDS, BONDS AND CDS

A **debenture** is a certificate given in acknowledgement of a debt. Debentures are bonds, usually without security, issued by a corporation. They may often be converted into common stock of the corporation, although many high-risk investment debentures provide no option for conversion. All you hold will be in effect a piece of legal paper, a promissory note with a term end and conditions of limitation of redemption.

Debenture stock is a debenture of a corporation or public company issued in the form of stock, the certificates of which are usually transferable but not redeemable. They entitle the holder to a perpetual annuity. The annuity is an allowance or income paid yearly or at specified times, often quarterly. These annuity payments are the return from an investment of capital in the corporation that is paid to the investor in a series of payments.

Dividends are a sum of money derived from profits or sales to be distributed among stockholders according to some predetermined method. There are tax benefits to receiving funds through dividends rather than through interest earnings.

In financial situations bonds are certificates of an obligation made under seal in which a person or corporation agrees to pay a certain sum at a specified time. Bonds are interest-bearing certificates of debt. They obligate the issuer to pay back the principal at a certain time. Municipalities, governments or corporations often issue them when they need to raise money to operate.

Certificates of deposit called CDs or GICs (guaranteed certificates of deposit) are documents issued by a bank showing that a person has a specified sum deposited with the bank. The bank uses these invested funds to place with loan seekers in order to earn income for the bank. The bank agrees to pay the CD holder a specified return based on the interest the bank earns from the deposit. GIC's are often based on funds that the bank has issued to mortgage holders. These types of investments have historically been considered very safe but are low in earnings. They are protected from loss by government legislated insurance protection up to a set value. In Canada the protection called CDIC (Canada Deposit Insurance Corporation) insurance is currently set at $100,000.00. In the United States this amount was recently increased to $250,000.00. EB1change sentence to read" specified return. The bank bases the rate offered on variables such as the bank's cost for money etc.

SAFEST INVESTMENTS

Safer government protected investments offer the lowest yields. Unfortunately in these troubled times some government backed investment treasury bills and bonds are no longer considered the safest of investments. It is more important nowadays to check out the financial viability of any institute in which you plan to place your investment dollars.

Putting all your money into safe investments means your money will likely lose in overall value over time due to inflation and income tax bites. It is not a good idea for long term investing to leave all of your funds in such vehicles. Interest income earned is also taxable in Canada except for interest on the recently introduced Tax free savings account. These accounts allow the depositor to put $5,000.00 each year into savings. Interest earned in this account is sheltered from income tax. There are withdrawal privileges. Through your broker you can also transfer a dividend paying stock into this tax free account thereby earning accumulated tax free dividends.

Following are basic descriptions only of types of investments. For details on any of these please refer to licensed financial planners or brokers. Jordan E. Goodman's book *"Everyone's Money Book on Retirement Planning"* provides an excellent full description of each type of investment as well.

Certificates of deposit (CDs) are offered by banks and credit unions. They allow you to lock in an interest rate for a specified period. If you withdraw your money before the term end, which may be three, six, nine months or a year or longer, there likely will be a penalty.

They are covered by government backed insurance protection up to $100,000.00 in Canada and $250,000.00 in the United States.

Cash can lose purchasing power value in inflationary times and is subject to theft or loss. There are cases of rodents using a stash of cash for their nests. Recently there was a case where a mattress with a million dollars secreted inside was accidently taken to the dump and not recovered. If you plan to keep cash store it in a safety deposit box at your bank or trust company.

Chequing account Some bank chequing accounts pay a small amount of interest provided the account maintains a minimum balance of $2,000.00 or more. However, unless you are a senior receiving free banking the bank charges applied per cheque issued or deposit made would offset any gains.

Guaranteed Income Contracts (GICs) are similar to bank offered CDs and may be purchased without a fee. They generally pay a fixed interest rate for a period of from one to five years. Each bank or credit union offering GICs will have a number of variations in their GICs available. There are cashable and non cashable types available as well. Some will have increasing interest rates the longer you hold the instrument. If investing in GICs it is wise to arrange laddered term ends. When first purchasing your GIC arrange each portion of the investment to expire on the first, second, third, fourth and fifth anniversaries. When each portion comes due reinvest it for another five year term. This will provide you with access to some of your money every year but eventually all your funds will be earning at the normally higher five year term rate.

Money-market mutual funds invest in a group of government or municipal backed or insured bonds. They are considered a safe type of investment. They may rise or fall in value with the bond market changes but over time may provide steady growth.

Savings accounts offered by banks and insurance companies often provide almost negligible interest income unless one opens a specific saving account type that provides higher rates. These may pay interest at rates comparable to GICs or more. Some will require minimum account balances of $2,000.00 to $5,000.00 to pay interest at higher rates. There may be restrictions on the number or type of transaction, or specific withdrawal charges. The interest may be calculated in different ways such as simple or compound, and are based on daily or semi- annual interest.

Treasury Bills have been considered safe investments. They are short term loans that you provide to the government on thirty, sixty, ninety and 180 day basis. Rates are in the GIC rate range. These are normally purchased through a bank on a specific day of the week.

LOW RISK INVESTMENTS

Low risk investments can provide a little more income than the safest level, while still largely providing protection of your capital.

Annuities are normally purchased through insurance companies to provide guaranteed income streams. Using actuarial tables, the insurance company establishes what the money will earn over time to determine the interest rate and pay back of capital. There are a number of types to select from. In exchange for receipt of a lump sum of money the insurance company agrees to pay out regular specified payments over a set period of time.

There are various plans and choices offered by insurance companies. When considering purchasing an annuity, look for a company that has a proven investment performance. It may continue to outperform other companies in the future. Depending on the earning power at the time of investment, your annuity investment may provide higher than GIC rates for the term of the annuity. My mother fared very well when she sold her stocks and purchased a locked in life annuity when interest rates were at 16%. EB4 is ok

In a variable annuity plan the payments received may be based on the earnings of the insurance company in its mutual fund investments. In this case pay out rates will vary over time. While you may earn at a higher rate there is more risk. If the company's track record warrants, a variable plan may pay out more than a fixed price annuity plan.

Straight life annuities cease making payments when you die. Your estate receives no benefit. Combination plans at lower rates of return are also available that can provide continuity to a survivor. Annuities can offer some tax benefits.

Blue chip stocks have historically paid out regular and often increasing dividends. These stocks are offered by long established companies that have taken the lead in their competitive niche of the market. Dividends are based on the corporation's profits and generally pay less than bond rates.

Convertible bonds hold a combination of both stock and bonds. As bonds they provide a lower dividend yield than straight bonds but combine with stocks for potential appreciation of the company shares. Depending on market conditions and the growth of the company stock held these may earn more than a GIC. However if the company's shares drop in value they will not perform as well.

Treasury Bonds – Government backed bonds allow you to lock in a set rate of interest over a long period of time. These bonds are not callable before maturity even if they are paying higher rates than currently offered bonds. They will be redeemable under certain conditions prior to their maturity date. Until recently they have traditionally been considered among the safest of investments.

Bond prices move in the opposite direction to interest rates. As interest rates rise bonds go down in value and vice versa. This occurs due to the bonds having been issued at a fixed rate that now may be less than the current interest rate as interest rates rise. Thus purchasers expect to buy bonds at a discount. Conversely when interest rates are low purchasers will pay a premium to purchase higher interest rate bonds that were previously issued while bond rates were higher. The longer the term to maturity of the bond the more likely it will fluctuate in value relative to interest rates.

Some bonds will provide semi annual payments of your interest. Others allow you to let your interest compound semi-annually receiving the compounded accumulated gain on maturity.

Bond funds - There are a variety of bond funds that can be considered. They may specialize in a certain type of low risk bond; government, municipal. Or moderate risk; corporate, global, etc. They may hold bonds in a specific short or long term maturity range.

Short term Bond funds - A fund holding bonds with maturities of up to ten years is considered to hold its value steadily since the rate fluctuations on holdings of shorter term bonds are less than rate fluctuations with long term bonds.

Life Insurance contracts - Except for term insurance some insurance contracts will accumulate a cash value in combination with providing insurance protection.

Utility stocks - Electricity, gas, water, sewage and some telephone company stocks are monopolies regulated by the government, providing service to a given area. As a result they have steady earnings and many will pay dividends. Funds made up from shares of these types of stocks will generally provide dependable income.

Zero coupon bonds - These bonds increase in value as they approach maturity but provide no interest payments. They are sold at a deep discount from their maturity face value based on yield value. If held to maturity they pay well because they have a specific schedule of compounding worth that grows until term end when the bond reaches its final stated value. Because they can be reinvested at maturity at the same rate they are attractive when interest rates are low. But in buying for long term growth a buyer gambles that interest rates will remain low. The down side of zero bonds is they react more to interest rate fluctuations.

MODERATE RISK INVESTMENTS

"It is gambling if you're just throwing money into a deal and praying."

Robert T. Kiyosaki

These investments will provide for mid range earnings since the level of risk is higher. Having some portion of investment funds in the moderate range generally enables an investor to gain on inflation.

Corporate bonds - Bonds issued by corporations introduce a level of risk since many corporations go bankrupt every year. For that reason they will pay 2% to 6% over government bond rates. Since bond-holders rank over shareholders interests in a bankruptcy, the possibility of loss even in a bankruptcy is reduced. It is important to check out the corporation's credit worthiness before investing. Does the company operate within a continuing favorable market? For example the development of digital imaging technology has made cameras that use film obsolete since there is no longer a market for the products. Also check out the pay back provisions that allow the company to pay back its bond before the due date.

Mortgage backed securities - Banks issue mortgages to homeowners and package a group of loans into funds that provide regular payments of interest plus paybacks of principle to the investor each month. These funds have been guaranteed by federal agencies in the past. Recently too many poor loans (sub prime loans) that went into foreclosure when real estate values plummeted were included in these funds, leading to the current recession.

Mortgage funds (Canadian) – Mortgage funds hold liens on a number of properties by way of registered mortgages. Canadian mortgage funds have traditionally maintained high equity to loan ratios with few foreclosures. These pay only the interest received so that your principle remains intact and can be redeemed with sixty or ninety days notice. They may create funds including only first mortgages, second mortgages or a combination called a blended fund. Each will pay a slightly different rate. Interest payments can be paid monthly or added back to your capital investment to compound your earnings over time. A long established fund with a large number of mortgages is a good bet for investment. Check how diversified their mortgages are and how current the mortgages are in their fund.

I have earned consistently higher rates on Canadian mortgage funds where the equity to loan ratio has been in the 35% range. This level of equity in the fund's mortgages has thus far provided adequate protection during the current downturn in real estate values.

Investment clubs – A group of people get together to pool their funds and invest as a group. Depending on their organizational structure and what they invest in these can be moderately risky or high risk investments. It depends entirely on how the club is administered, what the club invests in, and which risk category a specific club investment falls into.

Rental real estate – There are a variety of types of property to invest in. Among others the types include; condominium units, residential houses and duplexes, multi family buildings, resorts, and time-shares. Before purchasing, an investor needs to carefully study the rental market in the area they plan to invest in. They also need to determine how long they plan to hold the property. If you are thinking of investing in this arena, become knowledgeable about the investment area and its vacancy rate cycles, since these can adversely affect bottom line income. Market value may be partially established by cash flow value when the property is for sale again in the future. Keeping rents up at the market level will be very important to resale price. Be aware that disposing of real estate can take a length of time especially in soft market conditions.

The beauty of real estate investments in general is that while your actual out of pocket equity may have been low, the investment value increases based on the total value including any financing in place. You put your 5% -25% down but the property escalates in value based on the 100% value price. However, it will cost you to sell with an agent. This can wipe out your gains if you have only held title for a short period of time, dependant on market conditions. Plan to hold your property for more than a year in normal market conditions to realize any gain after deducting your re-selling costs.

Condominium units trade reduction of maintenance headaches for condominium contributions (commonly called condominium fees). An owner needs only maintain the interior of the unit since the fees pay for the exterior and common area maintenance. There are a number of types of condominiums. Most usual are residential apartment style and townhouse style, although warehouses and office buildings may also be condominiums. However, unless you can obtain a high enough rent it may be difficult at current market values to obtain a positive cash flow on a condominium purchase. Whether your unit is occupied or vacant you will still need to pay the monthly condominium assessment.

Time share ownership can be tricky. Some will be offered on 30 year leases rather than on a fee simple ownership basis. Their value will diminish over time as the years are spent. There will be high and low season weeks. You may or may not be able to rent your unit at times but will still have to pay your share of the management fees which can be quite high. While you may enjoy your holiday stays the time share ownership may not be a good investment vehicle.

Following chapters contain more details on real estate information.

Stock & bond mutual funds – These are investment vehicles that someone else manages for you to save you investigation and monitoring time. There now are many thousands of mutual funds to invest in through a large number of banks and brokerage firms. Many institutions will offer similar funds made up of groups of a specific type of stock or bond. Most funds do not outperform the market, especially during recessionary times. Look for low management expense ratio (MER) and good returns over time when selecting a fund. Certain industry groups will perform better than others at different times. A mutual fund broker can advise you by providing information that can assist you in making suitable selections to meet your goals. Investigate the mutual funds MER rate since a high rate will mean that you will need to earn that much more before your fund stock will grow in value.

Exchange Traded funds (ETF) EFT's are similar to mutual funds. They are made up of packages of investments tied to a specific stock exchange index. The index may specialize in a certain area such as banking, or the Dow Jones Industrial Average, or commodities such as gold or silver. EFTs are designed to diversify risk as well as opportunity. They often have a lower MER than mutual funds because they do not have to do the same level of market research since they simply track an index group.

CAUTION: When you are considering an ETF investment it will be up to you to do your own research, do your own evaluation and to make your purchase. When compared to a mutual fund supplier you will not receive the same level of guidance and service since ETFs are sold through discount brokerage firms.

Be careful since ETFs have become more popular they are now packaging them with double and triple leverage possibilities which immediately puts them into the high risk category instead of moderate to high risk area.

Chapter four discusses what to look out for when making condominium purchase investments.

CHAPTER 4

EVALUATING CONDMINIUMS

Boundaries; Evaluating a condominium purchase;
Reserves; Don't let bylaws & policies trip you up; New apartment
condominiums; Developer tricks; Be wary of rental conversions;
Bare land condominiums; Mixed use condominiums;
Condominium due diligence list.

My condominium experience was all gained in Alberta, where I managed condominiums for over twenty five years. I also wrote portions of the training course text books as well as magazine articles for the Northern Alberta Chapter of the Canadian Condominium Institute. In addition to heading my own management business, I served as a director of the Alberta Association of Condominium Managers.

CONDOMINIUM BOUNDARIES

Each province in Canada has its own condominium property act. There are variations in the laws detailing the development and administration of condominium corporations. In the early days of condominiums in Alberta, the boundaries between condominium units were set at the halfway point between adjoining walls of the units. Later it was deemed advisable to change the provincial laws to incorporate responsibility for the structure of the building in the hands of the corporate entity. At that time the boundaries of units became essentially the undecorated surface of the walls, floors or ceilings enclosing the unit. Then in Alberta with a few existing condominium corporation exceptions, windows and doors on the perimeter of a unit were also made into common property. The responsibility to administer common property rests in the hands of the board of directors.

EVALUATING A CONDOMIUM PURCHASE

"Do the study and analysis yourself based on your familiarity with the market.... If you don't have the familiarity, don't do the deal."

Keith and Sandi Cunningham

Low condominium fees do not necessarily mean that the condominium complex is a good buy. Before Realtors began to understand how to value condominiums, they would recommend complexes that had low condominium fees. However, what items are included in the fee structure need to be considered, especially the amount included for reserve funds.

It is true that a townhouse with its own private heating and water supply will have lower fees than those of an apartment, but the resident will have to pay these utilities separately. Townhouse owners may also have to maintain their own privacy area grounds keeping. In addition to providing grounds maintenance and janitor services, many condominium buildings will include water, heat and common area lighting in their condominium fees. Thus the utility costs to be paid individually by the apartment unit owner are reduced. Their fees may also include cable television or even in suite electricity. When making a cost comparison, it is important to tally up all elements of expense that the owner will pay.

A newer building may have lower fees than an older one because it has been built using high efficiency heating systems and low maintenance exterior finishes. However during the initial year or two of a new building it often happens that many developer deficiencies may come to light. The newer building may also be a longer commute to work when compared to the older building, thereby attracting a different rental clientele.

WATCH OUT FOR RESERVES

In Alberta the Condominium Property Act also sets requirements for condominium corporations to complete 'reserve fund' studies every five years. These are to determine how much money needs to be set aside for replacements of common property elements over the years. The goal is to establish reserve plans to provide adequate reserves to pay for replacements as required without special assessments. Unfortunately many existing buildings were caught with insufficient reserves. These buildings have had to incorporate special assessments into their reserve plans in order to meet their reserve fund guidelines.

The key element in evaluating a condominium purchase is the value of the reserve fund. Reserve funds are not paid back to owners when they sell their unit. They do however help establish the unit's value in the marketplace.

Unless the condominium complex has sufficient reserves to pay for the repairs and replacements necessary, the owner will be subject to a cash call; a special assessment over and above the fees. The age of a condominium will also make a difference to the reserve fund requirements. As a building ages various elements may require replacement, such as windows, patio doors, roofs, furnaces, plumbing lines etc. A low reserve fund virtually guarantees future special assessments will be implemented and these can be substantial. When buying a condominium unit it is wise to have your own personal reserve in your savings account.

DON'T LET BYLAWS & POLICIES TRIP YOU UP

Bylaws are the set of legal rules governed by the elected board of directors of a condominium. They spell out the legal agreement of all unit owners, stating the way in which the condominium corporation will be regulated. As soon as a person takes title to a condominium unit they are legally bound to comply with the bylaws that have been registered at government Land Titles for that specific condominium. In Alberta, in the event that no replacement bylaws have been registered at Alberta Land Titles, the bylaws given in appendixes to the Condominium Property Act form the legal bylaws. Many people have been confused about this point.

In purchasing a condominium it is important to thoroughly read the legally registered bylaws, the budget, the reserve study and plan, and review the corporation's financial position before releasing your purchase conditions. The bylaws may impose certain restrictions, such as age or numbers of residents, or pet restrictions that could affect the ability to rent. The bylaws impose legal restrictions that may be upheld in a court of law. Fines for the owner or tenant's non observance of the bylaws could eat into the owner's income. In many jurisdictions the board of directors of a condominium corporation has the authority to pass rules to make policies. Depending on the bylaw wording these may have the same legal enforcement ability as the bylaws.

Search the condominium additional page. If names have been registered it will tell you who the board of directors are, the service address of the corporation, and the date the last bylaw revision was recorded. If there has been a lien placed against the corporation it should also show up here.

Obtain a copy of the registered condominium plan. In addition to spelling out the unit boundaries it will indicate whether the attic space is common property or not. There will be a list of legal unit numbers accompanied by their square dimensions. The plan will also provide the unit factor for each unit on which the shares of common property ownership are based. These unit factors are used to determine your share of common expenses. In Alberta all condominiums must total 10,000 unit factors. Other jurisdictions may have other methods. In British Columbia condominiums are called strata units.

Since some expensive law suits can drag on unresolved for many years, you want to get information regarding whether the condominium purchase you are considering has any pending law suits in progress. Request an information sheet from the current management company or board of directors, if the corporation is self administered. Sometimes these are only sold as a package with an estoppel document.

An estoppel document is a legal declaration made by the corporation that indicates whether there is any debt owed to the corporation by a unit at a specific time. In condominium law the debt of unpaid condominium fees rests with the unit and whoever has legal title to the unit. Without checking thoroughly and requesting an estoppel document you could inherit the debt of the previous owner.

The information statement will provide information about legal cases, special assessments or other obligations. While many purchasers rely on their lawyer to obtain the estoppel package while preparing the closing documents, you may avoid unforeseen expense and problems if you obtain the information while your sale is still conditional.

In purchasing a condominium take all aspects into account in your evaluation.

NEW APARTMENT CONDOMINIUMS

"It is what you know that is your greatest wealth. It is what you do not know that is your greatest risk."

Robert T. Kiyosaki

A distressing fact has emerged over the years that applies to new construction condominiums. The budget prepared by the developer to assess condominium fees for the initial purchase will be based on developer's estimates. In order to appear more saleable the condominium fees will often be set much lower than the actual expense levels would indicate. In subsequent years the fees often will double as the actual operating expenses are realized. Keep this understanding in mind when you are planning your rental leases.

Because the building is new the reserve allocations may also be set at too low of a figure. If the reserve funding is not based on and adhering to an actual reserve study, the owners will discover in a few short years that they are behind financially and will need to catch up on their fund. Most often this is undertaken by levying a special assessment. Purchasers will believe they do not need much money for reserves since the building components are new and won't require replacing for a length of time. This kind of thinking may trip up a purchaser.

With a new building there are always additional expenses that are required to add the finishing items that the developer did not include. These may be the provision of a desk or office equipment, the addition of security cameras, the obtaining of special keys, the purchase of various maintenance equipment from vacuum cleaners and janitor carts to lawn mowing machines. Then there may also be unforeseen building problems related to the overall workmanship of the construction.

An area of concern when purchasing in a new condominium is the lack of accountability on the part of the developer. No one is looking out for the interests of the unit purchaser. People make the false assumption that local building code inspections ensure that the building is built according to codes. However, the building inspections are few. They may be limited to inspections of footings, framing, electrical and heating only.

WARRANTIES ARE QUESTIONABLE

Most new condominium units will be sold with a one year warranty. These warranty plans in Alberta have been set up by the builders for the builder's benefit. There are a number of exclusions to the coverage provided for elements of the common property. Also due to the length of time that units take to be sold, the common property warranty period may have already expired before an owner's board of directors has been elected. Therefore it is not unusual to have the expense of correcting common area construction deficiencies pass into the condominium owner's hands.

As soon as the board of directors is elected they need to obtain an opinion from the company providing the New Home Warranty about when the warranty period begins for the common property of their complex. Often the starting date has been set based on substantial completion of the complex. When the board takes control, this can leave a short time period remaining in the year's warranty period. For their own reasons some developers will not initiate the first annual general meeting and election of an owner's board of directors until the warranty period is already past.

DEVELOPER TRICKS

You could be surprised at what can turn up. In one building I administered, the developer was required by the municipality to provide a certain number of exterior parking spaces. Every unit was assigned one underground stall but some purchasers wanted a second stall. The developer created a scheme in order to get around the municipalities' requirements. He was attempting to make more money through sales of additional parking spaces. The developer installed several rows of high school type small metal lockers in a storage room. The small square of floor space of each locker was made into a legal unit with a title and was shown on the registered condominium plan. These titled lockers were sold with an assigned extra exterior parking stall for several thousand dollars. The purchasers mistakenly thought that they were buying parking stalls, but they were actually only buying storage lockers that included an assignment of a stall. Each storage locker was assigned a small unit factor share of ownership. That unit factor required the locker owner to pay a small monthly condominium fee. Eventually using their authority given in their bylaw wording, the owner's board of directors rescinded the parking space assignments except for several that had been mistakenly purchased by unsuspecting owners. The developer retained ownership of the unsold locker units and to this day continues to have to pay his share of the condominium fees.

BE WARY OF RENTAL CONVERSIONS

Watch out for rental conversions to condominium use. A developer may make cosmetic improvements to an old worn out unmaintained rental building to make it look in good condition to purchasers. They may paint the suites, replace appliances, and countertops and lay new carpet. They may place a small amount in a reserve fund to add to the market appeal. Hidden from view of an inexperienced buyer will be the need to replace the heating system, roof or plumbing system piping. The wiring may not be adequate for current usage. The fire system may need to be upgraded or the enterphone system replaced. Unless the reserve fund is large enough to cover replacement of the aging elements the purchasers will always have to fund cash calls. When buying a conversion it is prudent to engage a professional inspector to do an inspection of the building's common area elements.

Be wary if you receive an opportunity to become involved in completing the conversion of a rental building into condominiums. A re-developer may present you with glowing numbers about the funds you could realize by becoming a shareholder in the conversion. Taking part in the problems of a rental conversion is detailed more completely in the article titled 'Condominium Conversion Gone Wrong" in Chapter 13.

BARE LAND CONDOMINIUMS ARE DIFFERENT

Bare land condominium units have different boundaries than standard condominium units. Each unit is comprised of a parcel of land identified with survey stakes marking the boundary corners. When a structure is placed on the parcel it will not have any common property components. It may have a shared party wall if the structure is attached to another unit. Any underground services or irrigation provided to the bare land unit will also be part of the unit.

The bylaws for a bare land corporation will include a "managed property" component that provides authority for the corporation to undertake certain maintenance and insurance responsibilities on the unit owner's bare land parcel. Some roadways or park areas may be incorporated into bare land units that will be managed by the corporation, for which the corporation will pay property taxes to the municipality. Underground utilities, street lighting and roadways will need to be maintained by the condominium corporation at their expense.

MIXED MESSAGES IN MIXED USE COMDOMINIUMS

Mixed use condominiums are often those that have retail usage of the main or lower floors of a building and residential usage in apartments above. Both groups may share an underground parkade. Because the interests of commercial owners and residential owners are in opposition, there may be conflicts over the levels of maintenance and setting aside adequate reserves. Problems can develop between the commercial and residential owners. Unless the by-laws have been carefully written to fairly distribute the different types of business and residential expenses and to fund the reserves, there may be difficulties. The commercial unit owners will insist on keeping expenses to a minimum to enhance their profitability. They are concerned with their individual business's needs and security, but may have no interest in the rest of the building's needs. The residential unit owners will have a high priority for maintaining high maintenance standards since the building is their home. This type of building may be perceived as less desirable to rent as a residential unit unless tenants find the convenience of the building's location appealing.

CONDOMINIUM DUE DILIGENCE LIST

Request and read all of the pertinent condominium documents before releasing your purchase conditions. If you think the task is too onerous hire a knowledgeable person to complete the review for you.

INFORMATION /ESTOPPEL

1. Request the estoppel or at least the information statement for the corporation. If you are comfortable that there is no unusual debt on the unit let your lawyer order the estoppel just prior to closing.

2. Ask for at least a year's worth of board meeting minutes as well as the annual meeting minutes.

3. Obtain the condominium plan and review the unit factors and boundary statements registered on the plan.

4. Obtain and read the bylaws noting any questions to be addressed.

5. Obtain and read a copy of the management agreement.

6. Obtain owner occupancy ratio information.

7. Obtain and review the audited financial statement.

8. Obtain and review the budget

9. Obtain and review the reserve study

10. Obtain and read a copy of any policies or rules that have been put in place in addition to the bylaws

11. Get a copy of the approved reserve plan that provides the method of funding the reserves.

RESERVES:

1. How substantial is the reserve fund compared to the age of the building?

2. How soon will there be a need for funds to make major replacements?

3. Is this money in the fund already?

4. Is a cash call, a special assessment, likely in the near future?

5. Do you have a personal reserve or access to money for a special assessment?

BYLAWS & POLICIES

1. Do the bylaws allow pets?

2. Are their restrictions on ages of occupants?

3. Are there restrictions on the numbers of occupants in a suite?

4. Are there restrictions against renting to several unrelated parties?

5. Are there policies in effect in addition to the bylaws to be complied with?

BUILDING & AREA

1. What changes are you allowed to make, if any, inside your unit?

2. Is the adjacent area to the building being kept up or is it starting to get run down?

3. What kind of tenant is attracted to the area?

4. What is the owner to tenant occupancy ratio? (This can affect your mortgage raising capability.)
5. Is the building a conversion?
6. How old is the building?
7. How soon may basic elements require replacement? (Review the reserve study for details.)
8. Would the rent provide a positive cash flow?

LEGAL

1. Are there any outstanding legal cases?
2. Are parking spaces assigned or do they have separate titles?

Before proceeding to more complex types of investing it is prudent to learn how to read at least the basics of financial statements, as shown in the following chapter.

CHAPTER 5

EASY TO LEARN FINANCIAL STATEMENT BASICS

Reading financial statements; Balance sheet; Operating statement; Accrual method; Cash flow; Don't ignore record keeping; Update your budget; Gosh is that really my net worth?

Financial literacy is the ability to read and understand financial statements.

READING FINANCIAL STATEMENTS

I have been surprised by how few people can even understand a basic financial statement. For over twenty five years I dealt with many businessmen and women in their roles as directors of condominium boards. I began to realize how few of them understood what they were looking at when I gave them a financial statement. Yet being able to read and understand financial statements is critical to investing. Sadly schools did not teach this skill.

Unfortunately many corporate financial statements have become too complex. They are hard for an untrained individual to interpret and understand. This complexity can be attributed to tax planning and detailed methods of valuing assets and other business aspects. Aditionally, accountants are required to adhere to generally accepted accounting standards that a lay person may not understand.

The following charts and detailed summary provide just the basics of what is included in a financial statement. Honestly, it is not really that difficult to understand if you can get your mind around the basics.

The following chart is courtesy of FIC Investment Corporation and Gavin Radzick CFP.

The Balance Sheet

A business is created to make money by providing a product or service with the intention of creating a profit.

What the business owns or owes is reflected in the **BALANCE SHEET**

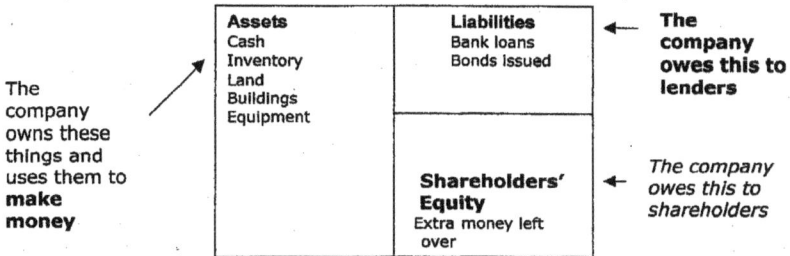

The company owns these things and uses them to **make money**

Assets	**Liabilities**	← **The company owes this to lenders**
Cash	Bank loans	
Inventory	Bonds issued	
Land		
Buildings	**Shareholders' Equity**	← *The company owes this to shareholders*
Equipment	Extra money left over	

This accounting tool has been around for 500 years. <u>A balance sheet gives a 'snapshot' of what shape the business is in at that moment.</u> The basic rule of the balance sheet is that:

Assets   =   Liabilities + Shareholders' Equity

Two things can happen to the profit. It can be paid out to the people who own the company (as a **dividend**) or it can be put into **Shareholders' Equity**.

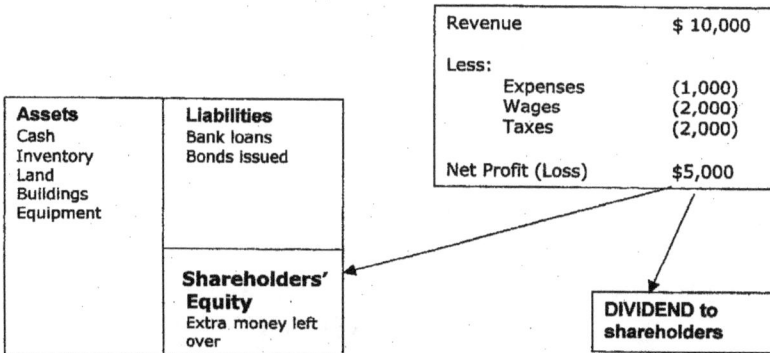

Revenue	$ 10,000
Less:	
Expenses	(1,000)
Wages	(2,000)
Taxes	(2,000)
Net Profit (Loss)	$5,000

Assets	**Liabilities**
Cash	Bank loans
Inventory	Bonds issued
Land	
Buildings	**Shareholders' Equity**
Equipment	Extra money left over

DIVIDEND to shareholders

If the money goes into Shareholders' Equity, it would likely be used to invest in more assets to make more money (hopefully).

57

"Financial literacy allows you to identify the strengths and weakness of any business"

Robert T. Kiyosaki

JUST THREE MAIN REPORTS TO MASTER

There are three main reports; the Balance Sheet, Income (or Operating) Statement and the Cash Flow statement.

The Income Statement lists current revenue and expenses based on a short period of time (called a fiscal period).

The Balance Sheet lists the cumulative position of the company over a long period of time, shown as assets and liabilities.

The Cash Flow Statement lists changes in working capital and dividends over a reporting period. Depending on the type of company there will also be additional reports.

"Financial   literacy is a vital skill if you want to build an empire."

RobertT. Kiyosaki

HOW CAN THE SAME INPUT INFORMATION PROVIDE DIFFERENT REPORTS?

INCOME STATEMENT + TIME = BALANCE SHEET

The Income Statement is a current record of revenue and expenses covering short spans of time, such as a month, quarter or year. It is a snapshot of the present moment.

58

The Balance Sheet records assets (property or resources held) and liabilities (or obligations) as a cumulative record covering the period since the business began up until the present day. It is a continuous picture of the company.

The same input information is used to prepare both the Income Statement and the Balance Sheet. In a double entry financial system the revenue and expense entries will be recorded as a plus to an Income Statement. The same information will be added using a minus to record it to the Balance Sheet. When the values are added to the prior year's totals it will show as accumulated assets and liabilities to date in the Balance Sheet.

The Income Statement will show the current gross and net profit as well as any current tax liability. The Income Statement may include comparisons to budgets or actual reporting periods of previous months or years. In some instances variances between Budget and actual figures may be shown either numerically or by percentage.

The current assets such as buildings, office equipment and furnishings, good will, money receivable, prepaid expense, inventory and their changes or depreciation in value over time will be recorded on the asset side of the Balance Sheet. The assets on the Balance Sheet may be separated into current and longer term assets.

The current obligations side of the Balance sheet will be categorized as current liabilities, longer term liabilities and shareholders equity. Accounts payable, short and long term debts owed, deferred taxes, and shareholders equity will be listed under liabilities. Shareholders equity as a liability, (or obligation) will include stocks issued and any retained earnings.

The total of all assets and the total of all liabilities including shareholder's equity will equal each other. By dividing the shareholder's equity by the number of outstanding shares and options the share valuation is realized as of a specific report date.

Every system of financial reporting records information derived from the company's expenses. Expenses include checks written, invoices paid, wages and benefits paid, loans or finance charges and options given to employees or directors as bonuses.

The revenue can be sales, interest earned, prepaid expenses, and accounts receivable. In a public company there may be a list of shares issued and options given as wages or bonuses. Asset depreciation, share and option valuations, and changes in inventory will be recorded.

WHAT IN HECK IS THE ACCRUAL METHOD?

The accrual method of recording is used to show accrued (accumulated) earned income and/or expense based on usage or cost attributed to a specific span of time. These accounts report revenue or expense that should belong to a specific period whether the money was received or is still receivable; or the invoice due was paid in that period of usage or not. An estimated journal entry will be made in the financial report and then reversed to record the actual expense when the invoice is received and paid.

For example in a full accrual method

- When interest on a long term investment may not be due within the fiscal period or fiscal year, the portion of interest allocated to that fiscal period is shown as earned.
- All prepaid expense (such as annual insurance) will be shown as a prorated monthly portion of the expense, as each portion is used even though the actual payment is made once for the whole year..
- All invoices paid will be prorated and applied to the fiscal period for which the cost was incurred. For example, utility billings would be reconciled to the month in which the usage took place

as opposed to the month in which the invoice was issued and paid. Any portion remaining for a subsequent period would be shown as a payable expense.

HOW IS MONEY FLOWING IN AND OUT?
= CASH FLOW STATEMENT

"When you're out of cash, you're out of business. Cash is truly KING."

Keith and Sandi Cunningham

The Cash Flow Statement records the actual cash that comes in as it flows through the reporting year or fiscal period. Since most record keeping is done on an accrual nature, this statement reports the actual timing of receipt of funds. The Cash Flow Statement shows whether more money is coming in than is being spent at any given time. Thus the money received is either creating a positive cash flow, or more money is being spent than is coming in. This change in flow will be very noticeable in seasonal businesses. If the cash flow is being generated only by the sale of shares or by the issue of credit that is not being collected, this can sound a warning note about the financial health of the corporation.

DON'T IGNORE RECORD KEEPING

Setting up a recording and bookkeeping system to track your revenue and expenses will be important when tax season rolls around. An open desk top box to hold legal file size pouch type folders enabled me to keep the expenses filed by category as the invoices came in. Each investment was set up with its own file in alphabetical order in which to place cheque stubs or correspondence. Each property had additional file pouches to receive utilities, repairs, caretaking and advertising. The file box holder was placed in a handy location by my desk where I could easily file the invoices as I dealt with them.

I avoided a huge headache at tax time by not letting my records accumulate in a jumble pile. At tax time I just needed to total each category, add my adding machine tape, and it was ready for the accountant. Accounting fees will be much higher if your accountant receives a shoe box full of mixed up receipts and records that they have to sort.

Deposit books were kept with copies of the actual deposit sheet attached to a deposit form in the deposit book provided by the bank. I kept a running account balance in my check-book register, including all checks written and deposits made even though many transactions were completed on line or at a bank machine. Separate bank checking accounts, lines of credit accounts and Visa cards were all maintained strictly for business use. For business purposes it was important to have the bank return my cancelled checks or as is currently done, photocopies of them. By not mingling the transactions with personal expenses I could then genuinely write off the interest and bank charges to expense. My comment: I guess I have to defer to American spelling of checks. Please search for others?

I kept Excel spreadsheets for the properties to track my rents due and any charge backs or interest due. My caretaker invoices were also standardized on the computer with hard copies filed in my file box.

I also kept individual files for each tenant with copies of any correspondence I had sent or received from them.

You may also want to consider setting up and using an accounting software package to record your transactions. Many are available, such as QuickBooks or Simply Accounting.

UPDATE YOUR BUDGET

Maintaining a constantly up dated budget on an Excel spreadsheet enabled me to determine how the expenses relative to a new investment, or changes in mortgage interest payments, etc. would fit in to my overall finances.

GOSH IS THAT REALLY MY NET WORTH?

"The true measure of wealth is net worth, not working income."

T. Harv Eker

Maintaining a current net worth listing on my computer was also useful. When going to finance an investment it was easy to print off or pull out appropriate figures for the lender's review package.

The following chapter discusses high risk investing and tips to gain more and lose less.

A basic rental spreadsheet follows.

Basic rent and deposit fourplex   Mar-06

Suite Number	Rent Due	Utility Deposit on hand	Security Deposit on hand	Name	Rent due	Previous Balance Due	Penalty NSF charges	Total due	Payment Received	Utilities Due	Utilities Paid	Balance (Overpaid) Underpaid
1	$715.00		$650.00	E R	$715.00			$715.00	$715.00	$240.56	$240.56 Paid to C for Feb	$0.00
1A	$575.00	$150.00	$725.00	C L	$575.00	$125.00	$25.00	$575.00	$815.56		($240.56) From T	
2	$725.00		Vacant		0							
2A	$725.00		$725.00	T S	$725.00	$125.00	$25.00	$875.00	$0.00		$900.00	
Total	$2,740.00		$2,100.00		$2,015.00	$125.00	$25.00	$2,165.00	$1,530.56	$240.56	$0.00	$900.00

E R lease ends.   June 30 2006
C L lease ends July 31, 06
T S lease ends February 28, 2006

Total rent $2,140.00

402 - The Aloah

Suite Number	Rent Due	Utility Deposit on hand	Security Deposit on hand	Name	Rent due	Previous Balance Due	Penalty NSF charges	Total due	Payment Received	Security Deposit due	Utilities due	Balance (Overpaid) Underpaid
412	$600.00		$400.00 ($400.00)	Tenant na[me] Returned security on move out	$600.00			$600.00	$600.00	$600.00	$0.00	0
Total	$600.00		$0.00		$600.00	$0.00	$0.00	$600.00	$600.00	$600.00	$0.00	$0.00

R L lease ends March 30 2006   Total rent $600.00

64

CHAPTER 6

HIGH RISK INVESTING

**Accredited & eligible investors; Risk acknowledgement;
Misleading sales tactics; Red flags; Investment seminars; High risk
investments; Proposal documents; Securities law;
Can you afford it?**

In order to invest in high-risk investments, there are security regulation requirements of eligibility to be met. These laws eliminate those who do not have sufficient income or sufficient net worth to be taking on risky investments where money could be lost.

ACCREDITED INVESTOR

To be considered as an accredited investor in some jurisdictions, you must have assets or income exceeding certain set values. To be accepted as an accredited investor you may need to declare financial assets with an aggregate realizable value before taxes, net of any liabilities, that exceeds $1,000,000.00. Alternately an accredited investor may need to declare an income before taxes that exceeds $200,000.00 for at least two years. Other alternate conditions to be met will be listed on the applicable application form. (*See details at end of chapter*)

ELIGIBLE INVESTOR

Depending on jurisdiction, eligible investors may need to sign a declaration that one has a net worth of $400,000.00. There may also be alternate conditions available in some cases. These conditions will be listed as appendixes to the offering memorandum.

RISK ACKNOWLEDGEMENT

A risk acknowledgement statement will also be required. On this form you acknowledge that you are purchasing a risky investment. You will be expected to sign your acceptance of statements that declare as follows:

1. I acknowledge that this is a risky investment.

2. I am investing entirely at my own risk.

3. No securities regulatory authority has evaluated or endorsed the merits of these securities or the disclosure in the offering memorandum.

4. The person selling me these securities is not registered with a securities regulatory authority and has no duty to tell me whether this investment is suitable for me.

5. I will not be able to sell these securities except in very limited circumstances.

6. I may never be able to sell these securities.

7. I could lose all the money I invest.

In Canada this statement may also appear: You have 2 business days to cancel your purchase.

MISLEADING SALES TACTICS

"Emotions, when mixed with unbridled greed produce economic disaster."

Keith and Sandi Cunningham

Salespeople will target a specific community or religious group. Once they get a prominent person in the group to invest it is easy for other group members to become involved through word of mouth. Having gained the trust of a core group of members the salesperson then may promote fraudulent services or products to the group.

In a bait and switch approach the investor will be introduced to a product that may be advertised or promoted as providing very high returns. Then when the salesperson meets the investor personally he switches the investor to another entirely different investment product.

Promises of sky high returns can lure investors. But registered brokers and financial advisors are prohibited by law from guaranteeing a rate of return on securities.

Seminars that offer a free meal or enticement to get you to attend are legal but in some cases once you are there a salesperson may be using the seminar as a ruse just to obtain your personal and financial information.

A salesperson may try to sell you unsuitable investments or get you to switch your existing investments into something he is promoting.

Some salesmen will prey on seniors using false or misleading credentials to imply that they have specialized training. They may use words like "registered," "certified" or "retirement" specialist in their titles which could be no more than a sales gimmick..

Unnecessary and/or excessive trades made on a client's account is called churning. It is done to make the broker more commissions.

RED FLAGS

Any of the following could be clues that the investment you are considering is exceptionally risky or even fraudulent.

1. Articles that give the appearance of news, but are actually paid advertisements.

2. Promoting above average or high returns as being no risk.

3. Providing loans to cover the investment cost and any future payment requirements.

4. Suggesting that you take the equity out of your home with a line of credit in order to invest in their scheme.

5. Promoting tax avoidance or moving money off shore.

6. Creating urgency to participate

7. Limiting the time an offer will be available.

8. Preventing enough time to obtain independent advice.

9. Promoting secret or exclusive techniques as unique.

10. Promising you will get rich quick or become a millionaire within several years.

11. Baiting then switching you to a variation different than what you thought you were investing in.

12. Misleading or contradictory statements made by sales people.

13. Offering a free flight to a property investment site where you will not be able to get independent advice before signing and could have to reimburse the fare if you do not purchase.

14. Requesting secrecy.

15. Paying finders fees for others that you bring in.

INVESTMENT SEMINARS

Many promoters will offer free seminars. A group of presenters will give self improvement talks and offer their products. The promoters will make their money by receiving commissions on any products or courses that the presenters sell. Be cautious about signing up for anything at these seminars as the energy can be highly charged and you will easily get caught up in the emotions and excitement. I have attended a number of these. At my first one I bought a program from all but one presenter. It was a waste of money because I did not have the time or energy to follow through on them all. At subsequent seminars I have learned a lot from the presenters and have been glad to be introduced to what they have offered. However, even though I am now wiser I still have a tendency to get caught up in the energy and take on more courses or pay for more information than I can handle. On the plus side I have met some really great business people, learned from some of the best trainers, and have benefited from investment opportunities.

HIGH RISK

"The successful people we admire are not the ones who made it.... We admire the ones who kept it."

Keith and Sandi Cunningham

While high risk investments offer the greatest potential for returns they also come with greater potential for losses. When you invest in high risk investments you must be able to afford to lose your money. In order to protect people from loss the government tries to limit who may purchase to those that have either higher income or higher net worth. Investors need to be wary of any investment opportunity that promises or guarantees a high rate of return that sounds too good to be true. This is the time to be skeptical and do your due diligence investigation. What is your gut feeling about it? Does it seem too good to be true?

Collectibles - Certain types of collectibles may retain a good escalating market value because of shortness of supply. Old masters paintings have appreciated well but other types of collectibles may not. Many things interest collectors; from coins to diamonds, from comic books to baseball cards. Some people feel that they can earn more through buying and selling collectibles than they can in day trading on the stock market. Thoroughly investigate the marketability of any group of collectibles before investing. Learn what to look for and what makes a specific collectible valuable. With baseball cards, for instance, fraud can be an issue. Investigate which firms can grade and authenticate your type of collectible. If collecting sports cards you may want to stick to those that have been independently examined, graded on a scale of 1 to 10 and sealed in protective plastic. If you need to sell your collectibles at auctions investigate the sales costs beforehand. A danger with collectibles is that you may want to hold onto your collection instead of buying and selling it to make money as a collection investor.

Commercial real estate - Opportunities exist to buy commercial real estate as part of a group, reducing personal capital investment. A purchase of commercial real estate can provide a tax loss write-off if the possession date is set in December with all take-over and legal expenses falling in one month. The owners group gains through holding the real estate for five years and then either selling or refinancing at that time to take out their equity. Investors receive quarterly payments of the commercial revenue. In accordance with completing due diligence, review the restrictions on selling your interest in the property.

As a high risk investment, realize that vacancies will reduce your income. You will also be locked into the investment based on the wishes of the majority of the group of investors. How competent is the leasing company? What is the track record of the development group?

Development projects – Many developers raise money through investors by offering bonds or mortgages to obtain funding for their construction projects. These projects may be condominiums, office buildings, commercial strip malls, etc. These high risk investments will pay top interest rates since carrying through to completion and sale is a risky long term proposition. Often these opportunities are offered through presentations. Conducting due diligence on the principals involved is absolutely crucial.

Foreign investments - These are risky since the way foreign governments administer business ventures is very different from North American methods. Very knowledgeable principals well versed in the foreign country's business methods and ethics must be involved for a company to survive and prosper. Even then surprising competition can quickly develop that may totally alter the value of your investment.

In my experience of foreign investing, I put money toward a venture in China. A very knowledgeable principal became conversant with the Chinese's way of doing business and set up business offices in a city in southeastern China. Before long land was acquired from the government and a factory was built with a plan to make a particular high demand supplement. The Chinese government allowed foreigners to take over land at a low cost provided they built a factory. But unless the factory became operational in a given period of time ownership of the factory would revert back to the government again.

Unfortunately a lengthy eighteen month delay occurred in obtaining audited financial information required for a Canadian securities commission. This postponed the company's ability to raise money to proceed to the next step of product production. By the time the lengthy audit procedure was completed the raw material source had been usurped by other Chinese people who had quickly built a competing factory. This effectively destroyed our company's marketing advantage.

Luckily due to the excellent communication efforts of the company's principal the government did not expropriate the factory. They allowed the company to sell it instead, thus sparing most of the invested capital, which was returned to investors.

Futures contracts - Commodity futures are traded on licensed exchanges by sophisticated investors and speculators. The investor agrees to buy a commodity months ahead of the actual sales price being established. The investor gambles that he is buying at a rate lower than his eventual sale. This market is high risk and very much affected by supply and demand. Commodities trading is not suitable for unsophisticated investors.

Junk bonds – These are high risk bonds in corporations that either no longer have high investment ratings or are too new to have been rated. They will pay from 2 to 10 percent higher than other bonds for that reason. Since the corporations could fail, the bonds could be downgraded in value and trading liquidity may dry up. Thus they are called "junk" bonds.

Mortgages – Investing your funds in a single mortgage greatly increases your risk. All your eggs will be in one basket so to speak. In the event of a down turn you may have to foreclose and take over ownership of the mortgaged home, land or business.

Options – Options provide an opportunity to leverage your stock purchase investment. You will need to set up a margin account with a broker. Option trading requires regular hands on trading as you buy and pre-sell contracts to purchase stocks at set prices. The advantage is that options may be purchased on leverage or margin. You take a gamble about the direction of movement of a stock price. If you guess wrong it can be expensive.

Raw land – Provides an opportunity to gain on growth of value as parcels of land are annexed to a city. Some companies offer opportunities to buy a share of a larger parcel with other investors. These will require long hold periods as a rule, often more than five to eight years to realize any gain. You will likely be required to pay the property taxes for your share of the parcel without receiving any revenue, so you will need funds to cover the negative cash flow. Depending on your agreement you may also be required to pay a share of design and utility servicing expense for future development plans.

"Land eats three meals a day."

Keith and Sandi Cunningham

Resort development shares - Opportunities are presented regularly to purchase shares in resort properties being built or offered in Canada, Mexico, the United States and other foreign countries. These are generally of longer term to realize gain. The opportunity could be to buy a building site or a share in a completed resort. It is important to complete due diligence not only on the principals offering the investment but on all aspects of the area, including the market, the laws, taxes, withholding taxes, government stability, construction, staffing, re-selling, and the return or repatriation of your capital etc.

SECURITIES LAWS

Securities regulations and laws, with slight variations in every one of 60 North American jurisdictions, cover every kind of trade. A trade is considered to be any transaction that involves shares, a debt instrument, right, warrant, note, option or mortgage involving corporate ownership or finance. Warrants are opportunities to purchase shares at a later date at a preset specific price. They are often bundled with a share offering to make the offering more attractive to investors.

While jurisdictions vary, the securities regulators will generally have the authority to impose fines, freeze the assets of a company from being sold, and ban from the market those principals who breach the securities acts. They can suspend a company's operations if financial information is past due its filing date. They can require disclosure of holdings, bankruptcies and interests of directors and principals. They often have the authority to levy fines of up to a million dollars for contraventions of the law. They may pursue offenders in court with the power to seek jail terms and fines up to five million dollars.

However, the securities regulator cannot get your money back. They cannot provide legal advice, investment advice, or comment on any investigation that is going on.

When it comes to private companies they are governed by less stringent rules of the local Business Corporation Act. When you invest in a private company don't be surprised if you as a shareholder receive sparse communication from them. There are no legal reporting disclosure requirements for a private company beyond holding an annual general meeting. Even something having a major impact on the shareholders may be withheld.

ILLEGAL TRADES

Do you realize that you could be involved and held accountable for an illegal trade? It is illegal to recommend investment in another's business venture if that investment opportunity hasn't been thoroughly reviewed to comply with securities legislation. I hadn't realized the full ramifications that the seller has a responsibility to ensure that the trade is legal and that the buyer is qualified to make the trade. The person making the recommendation is considered in effect to be a salesman for the investment or company.

TYPES OF PROPOSAL DOCUMENTS

When you are investing in a company you will be given an offering memorandum or a prospectus depending on the type of investment being offered.

A prospectus is the highest regulated level of disclosure. It is a very detailed and expensive to produce report that has been reviewed and vetted by both legal and securities authorities prior to approval to present to the general public. Every security must be sold with a prospectus unless the buyer qualifies for an exemption. Licensed brokers, family members, existing shareholders, directors, officers and employees of the company and certain sophisticated investors are examples of exemptions.

An offering memorandum is a less regulated document that does not receive prior review by the securities authorities. Once the funds being solicited have been raised, and the offering closed, the documents and the subscriptions will be filed with the securities authority for recording. But it will not be reviewed unless a problem is reported. The buyer is relying on management for compliance of the memorandum's statements. A subscription agreement and risk statement will be proffered along with an offering memorandum. A sample subscription agreement is included at the end of Chapter 13.

Private Placements in private companies are totally unregulated or controlled. They are often handled through a brokerage to sophisticated investors.

CAN YOU REALLY AFFORD THE GAMBLE?

"Leverage is borrowing a lot of money"
William K. Black

When our goal is to become rich there is a temptation to borrow too much money to invest in something we feel strongly about. Often gamblers buy stocks on margin accounts or leveraged accounts. When we have over extended ourselves with too much leverage our whole flimsy house of cards will collapse at the least little downturn. It is best to not spend more than you earn.

If you borrow to invest, use leverage wisely and affordably. When you buy securities using borrowed money, it will magnify the gain or loss on the funds invested. This is called leveraging. Here is an example:

You purchase $100,000 of securities or mutual fund stocks.

You put $25,000 of your available cash down

You borrow $75,000 to make up the difference.

If the value of the fund or securities goes down 10% to $90,000 of value, your equity has actually declined 40%. Your equity interest is now only $15,000 instead of $25,000. Your equity is the difference between the value of the securities and the amount you borrowed.

Make certain before borrowing that you are familiar with the terms of your margin or leverage agreement. The lender may impose a condition requiring that the amount outstanding on the loan not rise above an agreed percentage of the market value of the securities. If this occurs you would have to pay down your loan or sell some stocks in order to bring the ratio down to the agreed percentage relationship. For example:

You have a $75,000 loan on a $100,000 of investment securities.

The value of your securities declines to $90,000

Your loan agreement calls for a 75% relationship of loan to value.

You receive a margin call from your lender to pay down your loan.

You will have to reduce your loan to $67,500 (75% of $90,000)

Do you have a big enough reserve cushion? Remember that you also have to pay interest on your outstanding loan as well.

To obtain money to invest I decided to use a line of credit secured against my residence. Interest on the line was 5%. My investments were returning 16% and 18%, so I made 11% and 13% before taxes. I could also write off my interest expense to lower my taxes. But then one of my investments failed, a development I held a mortgage on went into foreclosure. If I didn't have other resources this could have cost me my home.

"Debt gives the illusion of wealth. True wealth is assets, cash flow and no debt."

Keith and Sandi Cunningham

CAUTIONS:

1. Borrow with caution. How will you repay it if your investment fails?

2. Can you read financial statements? In the beginning I knew little about financial statements, so I could not tell if a company was doing well or not. I didn't know what to look for. (See the chapter 5 on understanding financial statements basics.)

3. People like to tell you their investment tips, but be careful. Don't just rush out to act on them. Look into the opportunity first. Get enough information before signing on the dotted line.

4. Be wary. Many beginning investors rely on advice from friends. Where did their information come from?

5. Private company presentations try to get you emotionally involved to buy in. Sales presentation can be filled with hype and urgings to act now or you will miss out. Their offer with a limited time opening, or low one time only price is just a marketing ploy to get you to put out your money. Salespeople may exaggerate the potential.

6. If you do jump in and buy right away, be aware of the mandated cooling off period in your jurisdiction before your investment will be final. Often you can get out of the deal within 72 hours if necessary.

7. Make certain that you keep a copy of everything you sign. With the technology of copy machines and faxes it is easy to change a page.

8. Many of the opportunities out there for earning higher rates than bank rates are very risky. A risk statement specifically acknowledging that you may never get your money back may be presented for your signature along with an offering memorandum. The risk statement is your warning that there is no market for the shares or bonds that you may be purchasing and that you could lose all of your money.

9. Investors presume that there is some form of securities regulation protection. I know I certainly did. There isn't. Private investments are to a large extent exempt from the normal scrutiny of securities regulators or commissions. The private companies offering investment opportunities are not required to provide the same disclosure as publicly traded companies.

10. Don't be fooled by receiving an impressive looking offering memorandum that gives information about the investment. Since private companies are not subject to the same scrutiny by securities regulators that public companies are, the suggested high returns are not guaranteed. You are on your own. If in doubt, don't invest.

11. A publicly traded company is mandated to provide a prospectus, to disclose reports of material changes, to issue news releases and to provide regular financial statements

within a deadline-reporting period. While there is no guarantee that you will make money there are some protections in place for the investor.

12. Under what conditions can you redeem your funds? Some agreements will have a specified date. See my previous comment about chapter endings and do what is best.

Next I delve into renting real estate as an investment with its problem scenarios.

CHAPTER 7

DO YOU *REALLY* WANT TO BE A LANDLORD?

Financing my purchase; Selling myself to a banker; Tenants don't act like owners; Getting financing; Save grief – follow good renting procedures; Spend less on advertising; Pets can be a pain; Getting it rented on my terms; Rent verification form

"A great property manager is key to success

in real estate."

Robert T. Kiyosaki

DO YOU *REALLY* WANT TO BE A LANDLORD?

I was not a slum landlord. When I bought a property I would fix it up and try to keep everything in good condition. Some landlords, however, are only concerned with the bottom line. How much money can they take out of the property rather than how well maintained the property is for the tenants. Since I was keeping up the property I expected my tenants to respect my property. Did that ever create a learning curve! I was expecting others to live by my middle class values.

TENANTS DON'T ACT LIKE OWNERS

I should have remembered my own period of being a tenant many years before. My husband and I had sold our home to purchase an acreage parcel in 1970. We had a goal to build a new home on an acreage in the country. In the interim we had rented one side of a two story side by side duplex. Six of us and a dog moved in.

Where I would have cared for and repaired my own property, I spent no energy on keeping up the landlord's duplex. I was a careless tenant. The children marked up the walls and broke the gate. The dog's urine spots ruined the lawn. I did nothing about it. Why would

I bother, I was just a tenant. When kids in the other side of the duplex played their music too loudly or thumped noisily up and down the adjoining stairwell, in aggravation at the noise I would thump my side of the wall with a frying pan. No, I was not a very good tenant. I just didn't care enough. Living there was only supposed to be temporary.

How a person relates to property when they are a tenant versus being the owner is very different. Having been both an owner and a tenant I should have known the difference in attitude between owning and renting.

One day after having been a landlord for a few years I realized I did not relate well with certain kinds of people. Their life styles and values were so different from mine. Had I recognized that earlier I would have purchased other types of rental properties, such as single homes that would attract a different type of renter.

FINANCING MY PURCHASES

Not planning to live in the rental properties I was buying, I knew I would require larger down payments. Where an owner occupier could buy with 5% down, as an investor I had to put down 35% of the appraised value to obtain new mortgage financing. As a single woman not earning a huge salary, it was sometimes hard to get adequate financing. A good mortgage broker was indispensable to me. He knew which lender was the most amenable to lend to me, dependent on the current market circumstances at that time.

When it was possible to purchase with a low down payment, I would assume an existing mortgage with a vendor take back or second mortgage.

When I bought the rooming house with new financing I had to have a second person qualify with me in order to satisfy the mortgage lender. My employment income was low and my rental incomes were discounted by the lender. After a year I was able to remove the qualifier from the title.

After spending too much time driving to my rentals which were spread in distant corners of the city and a nearby town, I decided to only purchase properties nearer to my home. This saved me hours of time spent driving to and fro, plus the cost of fuel.

SELLING MYSELF TO A BANKER

As my portfolio grew, I followed the instructions received at R.E.I.N. (Real Estate Investment Network) to create a financing book. In a small white binder I placed all the information that bankers would require in order to make a positive decision to lend to me. The first page was a description about me and my ultimate investing goal plan. The next page was a copy of the listing for the property with a picture. Third would come a copy of my conditional purchase agreement, then a copy of the property's title. In following pages I listed my net worth statement and my proforma plan for affording the new property. To verify my income I included an employment verification letter from my employer plus copies of all my existing leases. I knew the fussy banker would also want copies of my last two years of tax returns, so they were also included. From my experience, I recommend making copies of the pertinent sheets so they are available for your next financing book.

Due to my organization, the banker had all the information he needed except to order an appraisal of the property. Banks normally only accept appraisals from the bank's authorized list of appraisers, so I had not preordered a market value appraisal of the property.

The first banker I gave a financial binder to was totally surprised. Smiling, he said he had never received such complete information. I quickly was approved for the mortgage loan.

When the bank sends out an appraiser they are looking for the appraiser to provide a value that indicates that the bank's loan on the property would not exceed their percentage of equity to loan limit guidance. If the banker gave the appraiser the property purchase price the appraiser would often just insert that number as the appraised value, regardless of what the actual market value might be. I sometimes chided the banker that their appraisals were biased.

SAVE GRIEF - FOLLOW GOOD RENTING PROCEDURES

It was a drag but I read through all the clauses of the Residential Tenancies Act. I learned about tenant rights and my rights. The city Landlord and Tenant Advisory Board sold me rental leases, condition reports and other useful forms. Some forms were also available from R.E.I.N. and Wright Thurston's courses I had taken. Long before as a Realtor I had learned how to prepare contracts.

I signed up for a Rentcheck credit reporting account. They provided reports from several credit reviewing agencies like Equifax that I could order online at minimal cost.

SPEND LESS ON ADVERTISING

Initially I would place signs in the window and ads in the newspaper as well as notify student housing at the university. My vacancies were listed as non-smoking spaces. When I placed newspaper ads I learned that adding a one line catch phrase in a classified ad would help me rent faster. One line in a four line ad I used to rent my rooming house was "A friendly place to call home" It seemed to attract more family oriented people.

For renting a 2000 square foot luxury condominium I wrote an emotionally descriptive paragraph to help me rent it. Where the four line classified ad for the rooming house used a number of acceptable word abbreviations, the longer paragraph did not. Again the ad stood out from others and cost more but it attracted the right kind of people.

For my rooming house I did not want to spend much on newspaper ads since I had to place adds so often. There is a large turnover of tenants in a rooming house. I tried placing ads in the bulletins of several nearby <u>stores</u> but they didn't reach any potential tenants. My tenants were coming from other than the local areas. Some were students so I also placed ads with student services directories.

When I placed an ad in the newspaper I did allow an extra fourth line that helped to attract better tenants. My sample four line ad with a bold address did not give the actual address but narrowed it to a particular area. I used only readily understandable abbreviations. SD is security deposit and NS no smoking. Later craigslist.org, Rentright.com and Places4Rent.com came into being. I found the latter two to be very effective at much lower cost.

> **1000 St. 80 Ave** "A friendly place to
> call home" bright furnished rm. incl: fridge/
> cable/ph/util. share kitch. & new baths,
> near bus $000/mo. SD $000 NS 480-3700

PETS CAN BE A PAIN

I took care when I rented my spaces out. I didn't rent to people with pets unless I took a pet damage deposit. I had learned the hard way that cat urine and its clinging odor may mean that I would have to replace my carpet, underlay and any drapes that were used as scratching posts. Dogs were no better. They damaged doors by scratching with their untrimmed claws to get outside. The owners seemed oblivious to their dog's barking. Dog calling cards would collect in growing heaps all over the lawn becoming an unsavory mess to be cleaned up. I didn't relish calls from the angry neighbors either.

GETTING IT RENTED ON MY TERMS

"It is virtually impossible to rent out a larger house for enough money to cover the mortgage payments. Therefore it is wiser to stick with the cheaper property where rents and mortgage payments are more in line."

Robert G. Allen

Tim Johnson taught me to book my rental showing appointments one after the other about 15 or 20 minutes apart. One prospect might be filling out their application in one room and another could be finishing their application in another room. I would collect cash deposits from each applicant, notifying them that they would be advised the next day whether they were accepted or not. The next several prospects would also be given applications for a waiting list if they were interested. A prompt refund would be given as soon as the checking was completed and a selection was made.

If an interested applicant filled out an application form I would review it briefly with them. I watched to see whether their incomes looked sufficient to carry the rent and whether there was enough information to do a reference and credit check. If they were interested I would collect a cash down payment toward the security deposit.

Then I verified their information. I would contact personal and employment references and complete a credit check. By telephoning two previous landlords I would find out what kind of tenants the applicants had been. I would ask:

1. Are XYZ tenants good tenants?

2. Do they pay their rent on time?

3. Do they have any pets?

4. Do they keep your place clean?

5. Have you received any noise complaints about them?

6. Had they given proper notice to vacate?

7. And the crunch question: Would you rent to them again?

Every effort on my part to only accept good tenants was worth my time. But, however much I thought I was doing to protect myself, I still made mistakes in tenant judgment on occasion.

Booking showings for one property on the other side of town a 45 minute drive away caused me much wasted time and grief until I used a tip from Tim Johnson. Tim used to make an appointment for a property showing, but tell the prospective tenant that he would not meet him at the property unless they called Tim a short time before the appointment time to confirm that they would be there. No call, no showing. To spare himself two trips Tim also made sure that both husband and wife would be there together oor he would not book a time until they could both be available. For that property across town I also insisted on a year's lease instead of my usual six months.

If there was any problem with the application information I learned to turn the applicant down and return the deposit. Initially I did not take a deposit before screening potential tenants. I would spend my precious time and money to do the check only to find out that the potential tenants had changed their minds. If I let them give me a check I might discover to my sorrow that it would not clear the bank. Then I had to start my tenant search all over gain.

I carried a set of necessary application forms, leases and condition reports along with a duplicate receipt book in my car to be certain that I had what I needed for every showing.

Once accepted, the tenant would be asked to pay the balance of one month's security deposit in cash, along with the first month's rent. In most cases, the tenants would sign a minimum of a six month lease. I was careful to get the names and signatures from all the prospective tenants if more than one adult person would be living there. I wanted to hold them all responsible for paying rent.

The carpets would be cleaned before a tenant moved in. The tenants would initial the lease clause stating that it was their responsibility to clean the carpets when they left. The tenants also signed shared utility agreements where applicable. It was mandatory that the tenants also signed to acknowledge that the smoke detector was in working order.

I would have them initial the insurance clause that stated that they were responsible for their own tenant insurance package. As the property owner, this was necessary for my protection from insurance claims that might arise within their rented space. Many tenants never take out tenant insurance on their possessions. They almost never think to obtain liability coverage to protect themselves from liability damage claims that could arise from their negligence should a guest of theirs have an accident within their rented space.

After I had experienced several late rent episodes I added penalty clauses to my lease agreements. A per diem charge was added for late rent.

When tenants moved in or out I completed a three part detailed condition report with them and made certain that they signed it and received their copy. The first original copy was then used when the tenants moved out.

RENTAL SUMMARY POINTS

1. Tenants treat properties differently than owners

2. What strata of population are you comfortable renting to?

3. Pets cause damage. Take pet deposits

4. Use mortgage brokers

5. Assuming with vendor buy back agreement

6. Will you need a qualifier to help you purchase?

7. Investing close to home saves travel time

8. Become conversant with contract wording

9. Keep several year's copies of your income tax returns to show to lenders

10. Create financing book to give to bankers:

   - Develop your statement of goal purpose
   - Prepare your net worth statement (Update it regularly)
   - Include listing information about the property you are buying
   - Include a copy of the title
   - Prepare a proforma for the property to be financed
   - Include a verification of income statement from your employer
   - Include copies of any existing leases or tenant signed rent verifications
   - Include copies of two years of tax returns
   - Make copies of the pertinent sheets for future use

11. Study the Residential Real Estate Act for your area

12. Obtain any necessary rental forms:

- Application to rent
- Lease contracts with addendum of rental conditions
- Condition inspection agreements
- Security deposit return forms
- Eviction forms
- Utility responsibility forms
- Smoke detector forms
- Pet registration agreements

13. Arrange to obtain credit checks
14. Advertise in newspapers or on the internet
15. Write your advertising to attract tenants
16. Obtain window signs with your telephone number
17. Create occupation rules if necessary
18. Prepare property, clean carpets, paint etc.
19. Booking rental appointments:

- Have receipt book and forms handy
- Take cash not checks with rental applications
- Take multiple applications
- Get names of all potential tenants

20. Check references from; prior landlord, employer and personal
21. Obtain a credit check
22. Return deposit to unsuccessful applicants
23. Sign lease agreement
24. Sign addendum of rental conditions with all tenants

25. Have tenant initial insurance clause, penalty clause and other important clauses

26. Fill out additional forms for utilities, pets or smoke detectors etc.

27. Complete inspection with tenant and both sign condition form

Make certain your tenants know how to reach you. When they move in it is very good for personal relations to take a small impersonal gift, like a box of donuts, or case of Pepsi, or perhaps a chicken take out dinner for the family.

NARROW ESCAPE FROM AN OLDER APARTMENT BUILDING

My first incursions into real estate began while I was still married. In 1975 before my divorce, my husband and I purchased a three story older apartment building with six suites. It had an attractive tan brick exterior that looked trouble free. It was in a preferred quiet neighborhood and in close proximity to the city center. The apartments were occupied by long term tenants. The suites had old outdated pink and turquoise built-in counter top and oven appliances. These should have warned us about replacements that would be needed, but our eyes were glazed with the overall attractiveness and excitement over the great location of the building. When we toured the building we were only shown a few suites. We did not see them all.

Since the vendor owned the building with clear title it was necessary to raise the purchase capital by placing a new mortgage. At that time it was relatively easy to arrange with both of us being employed.

The tenants, mostly seniors, had been in the building a long time and were paying very low rent. For many years the vendor who owned the building outright had not raised any rents even though rents were now considerably higher. We learned that some tenants had been living there almost twenty years without an increase. When we took possession we gave everyone a $70.00 increase in rent. We needed the money to pay the mortgage payments. The upset tenants came down on us like a ton of bricks. A $70.00 a month increase was huge at that time in 1975.

OH OH! RENT CONTROLS

In times of tight rental markets governments will pass rent control laws that restrict how much or how often you may give rent increase. Unfortunately there are more tenants than landlords that vote and can sway the government's decisions. Rent control interferes with the natural supply and demand market place causing distortion in availability of housing supply. By protecting tenants from market rents the government stops the supply cycle. Landlords will not add more units to the supply unless they can be profitable.

Unknown to us, on the very day that we removed our purchase conditions on the building, the government had passed a rent control law. They limited rent increases to 5%. Our rent increases of $70.00 a month were certainly higher than that. The angry tenants objected to the rent control department of the government. We in alarm appealed our circumstances to the rent control investigator. Without the increase in rent we would have to subsidize the building by over $715.00 every month, a large sum for us in those days.

In addition we would have to begin renovating the building. By now we had realized sadly that many of the outdated appliances needed to be replaced. The Fire Department had recently passed a new law that also required the installation of smoke detectors in every suite. We were faced with added expense on top of the mortgage payments that we hadn't counted on. We were becoming apprehensive. We just didn't have enough extra money available.

The rent control board turned down our appeal. We were really alarmed now. How could we possibly cover the payments and growing list of repairs? Our only option was to find a buyer to quickly purchase the building from us. Because of the great location we did sell right away, thank goodness.

The rent control legislation was so new that these buyers had also not realized that they would be prevented from increasing the rents. I think it must have been about 5 years before that purchaser was able to raise the rents sufficiently to cover their mortgage payments. In addition all the appliance replacements, cupboard renovations and smoke detector expenses came from that purchaser's pocket as well

EXPENSIVE LESSONS

1. Look carefully before you leap. A great location isn't everything to be aware of.

2. Inspect every suite. List all the required renovations that you can spot. Then price them before removing any purchase conditions. If the expense is larger than you anticipate ask for a reduction in your purchase price.

3. Have a professional inspector look into the condition of every suite, of the boiler room, and roof etc. This is especially important with an older building.

4. Have the Fire Department inspect the building for any required upgrades needed to comply with the current laws.

5. Watch for out of date types of appliances or other fixtures. If old, built-in style of range tops and ovens are no longer available, you may need to replace cupboards as well, to be able to install a slide-in range. Or if the appliances come in a special size like 24 inch apartment stoves used to, you may

have to replace them with the now more standard 30 inch width. Is space available to fit the larger appliance dimension?

6. With an older building purchase take into account items that will need to be replaced in the future. Things such as windows, boilers, water tanks, roofs, paving etc. can be nearing the end of their life. Replacements can be very expensive. That potential expense may be the very reason the present owner is attempting to sell the building.

7. Watch for loose tiles or missing or darkened caulking in the bathrooms. The grey color on the caulking may indicate that mould is developing behind the tile walls. Mould restoration can be very expensive.

8. Plan for unanticipated expenses especially if you are buying an older building. Set aside an adequate repair fund or arrange an adequate line of credit to fall back on if necessary.

9. Check into things like rent control. Is there any legislation that prevents rent increases or limits them to a small percentage each year? Are there restrictions that limit how many rent increases may be made each year? If you need to bring your rent revenue up to market rents how many times a year can you give rent increases?

10. If you anticipate keeping existing tenants, have each tenant sign a rent verification form. On it have a clause asking them how long they have been living there. Are they renting on a month to month basis or do they have a current lease? When does the lease, if any, expire? Another clause could ask when they had last received a rent adjustment. To obtain financing your lender will require this information.

11. When raising rents be considerate of your tenants. What is a reasonably affordable rent increase that you can impose without losing good tenants?

In Chapter 8 rooming houses as investments are highlighted along with their problems.

Rental form follows:

RENT VERIFICATION FORM

We/I,_____living at

#_____ at _____, _____ are

currently paying a monthly rental of $_____. We/I also

have Paid as a security deposit $_____

The rental/lease agreement we have signed expires on

_____

Date and time

The contract is for a period of _____months/days

The number of people living at this address is _____ adults &

_____ children. We/I have the following pets:

_____

Under the terms and conditions of our contract, we/I pay the

following utilities:

Power___Water___Sewer___Waste___Cable TV___Telephone___

Other_____

We /I have/ have not paid a last month's rent, the amount being $

_____

The furniture in our residence, listed below, belongs to the owners of

the building/apartment: (list item and condition)

_____

_____

_____

Use the space on the back of this sheet as needed.

We/I have indicated below any special arrangements made with the owners/managers:

_____

_____

Signature of all adult residents:

_____

_____

_____

_____

Dated at _____ on _____ 20____

Signature of owner and /or representative

_____

Date

_____

CHAPTER 8

ROOMING HOUSE HEADACHES

Upgrading the building; Tenant foibles; Tips and expensive lessons, Cash flow analysis; Rooming house forms

"Regardless of the time. real estate is a necessity. People need to live somewhere; in a house, an apartment building ,a condominium, a townhouse, a trailer park.
They have no choice."

Robert G. Allen

ROOMING HOUSE HEADACHES

I made many mistakes when I bought a rooming house not far from the University. Whatever was I, a lady who had grown up in relative comfort, doing with such a purchase? I had no understanding of the kinds of people situations that I would have to face. I only saw the money potential. If after taking in this story you still wish to own a rooming house I recommend that you know the type of tenants you will attract and whether they will fit your own personality.

The revenue to be earned looked attractive since it provided a good positive cash flow. But the experience of running a rooming house proved to be quite trying at times. Without the excellent services of a trusted lady friend who became the live in caretaker, I would have been in serious trouble many times over the nine years I held the property. In my innocence I had no idea what I was getting myself into.

I had purchased a thirty year old two story brick and stucco faced house with a raised basement, four full four piece bathrooms, three kitchens and nine bedrooms on a narrow lot. There was also a small laundry area in the furnace room. The double garage had two parking spaces on its driveway on the rear laneway. The upper floor contained four bedrooms, two full bathrooms and a small kitchen. The main floor was a suite for the caretaker plus storage room and one rented room. The lower level had three bedrooms, another kitchen and a bath as well as the furnace laundry room.

UPGRADING THE BUILDING

Excited and pleased with the building, I wanted to get it into top shape for the tenants. I had saved out $20,000.00 for repairs. A new roof was installed and extra attic insulation blown in. One of two furnaces was replaced as well as a large commercial water tank. The inventory of furnishings was outdated. Most of the furnished rooms required complete rehabbing. I found a good second hand furniture store where I bought tables, chairs, lamps, and mattresses. Bed-in-a bag purchases along with new pillows supplied the needed replacement bedding. Several new small room fridges were purchased to replace the oldest ones in several rooms. Walls were painted, pictures were hung in the hallway, and carpets were cleaned. My caretaker moved in and I was in business. I even had art pieces hung on the walls of each room.

PURCHASE ERRORS

Then my spirits sank as I learned that the purchase information supplied by the secretive Realtor was missing a vital document. This was a denial to a previous owner's request for rezoning to allow rooming house use. The building was apparently zoned only for use as a duplex even though it had been operating for many years prior to my purchase as a 9 bedroom rooming house. I learned later from an appraiser that many years ago a previous owner had professionally added a second story to the building to create the duplex into a rooming house. This explained why the house looked like it had always been a rooming house. But it was actually an illegal usage.

It was upsetting to find that out. Of course I didn't learn about it until some time after my purchase conditions had been removed and my purchase was complete. Had I known in advance that it was an illegal usage I might not have purchased. Owning illegal properties can bring many headaches, which this odd building certainly did in the end.

I had also erred when I accepted an out of date real property report that did not show fence lines. A real property report is a type of survey in which all auxiliary structures, such as fences and garages on the land parcel are also included. Newer reports now include them. The report I received didn't show that a metal fence post encroached on the city land. I paid a $40 fee and sent in a request for an encroachment agreement. Eventually the agreement was executed and arrived with an invoice from the city for $400.00. Had I even asked ahead or realized what the cost would be it would have been so much cheaper to just have shortened the fence a foot.

The neighbors on one side, I discovered when I met them, had had a poor experience with the previous owner's student renters. They let me know right away that they would not tolerate excess noise or too many parked vehicles on the street before they would complain to the city. They knew the usage was illegal, and that I was at risk of being shut down. I cautioned my caretaker who was very careful when selecting tenants after that. Because my garage and parking pad only accommodated four vehicles, she rented mostly to people who used public transit instead.

When I purchased I accepted the previous tenants in residence. I had even made it a condition that all rooms be occupied at possession time. I thought I could not afford the vacancies and lease costs while I found my own tenants. However, the vendor's careless caretaker then rented the empty rooms to several unsuitable tenants and oh boy did I inherit problem people.

STORAGE EQUALS EXTRA REVENUE

To make extra money I rented out one side of the double garage. The other side was for the use of my caretaker. Each quarter of the remaining space was given a rental value and the space was rented to other people, not the tenants of the rooming house. These people would sign a rental agreement, make a stack of their belongings in an assigned area, and receive a key to the garage. This was bringing in easy extra revenue, or so I thought. That was until someone's old stored mattress and belongings attracted mice. Then mice pellets took away some of the gravy.

Even though all the tenants were required to sign lease agreements and a set of rules that banned smoking or drinking, some would smoke or drink in their rooms anyway. These were the rules:

Occupancy Rules for:

(Name)_____

I_____ hereby agree to be
bound by the following occupancy rules for residence in room #
_____ at _____ , _____.

1. All rent payments are due on the first day of the each month in
    advance. All payments received after that date are delinquent and
    accrue a late charge of $10.00 per day until overdue balance is
    paid.

2. If rent has not been received by the third day of the month an
    eviction notice will be given.

3. All returned checks are subject to a $25.00 service charge. Any
    returned cheque must be covered by cash or a certified cheque or
    money order.

4. Rent payment is to be made to the caretaker, Sharon Scott, at her
    residence on the main floor prior to noon on the first day of the
    month.

5. No overnight guests or pets of any kind are allowed.

6. No smoking is allowed inside any portion of the building.

7. The keeping and usage of any, and all kinds of hallucinogenic
    cigarettes or drugs, and excessive use of alcohol, are prohibited in
    the building or on the grounds.

8. No noise is permitted after eleven P. M. Please be thoughtful of your neighbors and do not disturb other residents with excessive noise from your stereo or television.

9. Personal items may only be stored in the garage with the permission of the landlord.

10. I agree to give one month's notice in writing if I decide to vacate the premises.

11. I agree to clean up after myself when I use the shared kitchen, laundry room and bathroom, and to wash all pots and dishes immediately after usage.

12. I agree to wipe up any spills, I may cause in the shared bathroom. I agree to periodically clean and vacuum the carpet in my assigned room.

13. I acknowledge my responsibility to compensate the landlord, by deduction from my security deposit, for any damages done to the furniture, bedding, and / or the premises by myself and / or my guests.

Dated at _____this ___Day of _____20____

Tenant copy received: _____

_____   _____   _____

Witness   Tenant   Room #

TENANT FOIBLES

Some of the following incidents may give you a chuckle.

One young man from India who lived there several years became a pack rat. He seldom opened his door more than a crack if the caretaker knocked on his door. After several years it was discovered that his room was filled to the door with possessions leaving barely enough space to walk in. He had filled the room, enclosing even the bed with shelving units filled to the ceiling. His window fire escape was not even accessible. He was given a stern ultimatum. In order not to be evicted he agreed to remove many of his possessions. He was provided with storage space in the garage for an increased rental fee. The garbage bins were also nearly overflowing for a while.

When his room was cleared enough to get to the window, our inspection of his room also brought to light a colony of fruit flies clustered and flying around the window. Apparently he had also kept food in his room that had attracted them. We gave him the cleaning material and insisted that he remove them immediately.

This same young man, I will call Pack, used to use his computer and equipment in his room a lot. He didn't have enough outlets he said. One day I discovered he had run electrical wires along the hallway floor to plug his equipment into the kitchen fridge socket. Of course the cords were a tripping hazard. When he was asked why didn't he use the outlet closer to the door of his room, he replied that the vacuum cleaner disturbed his computer when both were plugged in at the same time in that double outlet. He was ordered to relocate the wiring above the intervening doors.

One day Pack bought a used red station wagon and parked it in front of the house. It stayed there for days and eventually the license expired. He said there was something wrong with the vehicle but he could not afford to get it fixed or to buy a new license. The caretaker hounded him; the other residents complained that he was taking up usable parking space; but still he did nothing. Even the next door neighbor complained about it. After many warnings went unheeded, the caretaker finally persuaded the city bylaw officers to ticket it. When Pack still took no action, the bylaw department finally had it hauled away, but months had gone by.

One middle aged man took a strong liking to the caretaker. He would slip love notes under her door almost every day. She was so glad when he moved out after her numerous rebuffs of his advances.

During a room cleanup from a tenant who had skipped paying rent, the caretaker and I were dismayed to discover the mark of an iron burned into the carpet.

Another chap from the Middle East took the sheepskin mattress cover from his queen sized bed and placed over the windshield of his car. He hooked it in place over the two side mirrors. When he was accosted by the caretaker he said they did that all the time in Iran. It was to keep his car warm in the winter. The caretaker hustled him back inside with the mattress pad.

If it was not one thing it was another. There were always situations to be addressed.

One time water was discovered dripping into the storage closet on the main floor. When the caretaker went upstairs she found the kitchen sink overflowing. One of the young men had forgotten to turn off the tap when he went to answer the telephone.

At least I had been smart enough to have the telephone company place a toll restrictor on the common telephone line in each room. It prevented anyone from making distance calls at my expense.

While my caretaker and cleaner took care of the kitchens, bathrooms and hallways, all tenants were to clean their own rooms and wipe up after themselves in the kitchens. One original tenant on the lower floor was a sweet old man with autism, I will call Tommy. He was living on an assisted living allowance. His neighboring resident, also on government assistance, was a depressed man who I will call Brad. Brad couldn't bring himself to find work. We later learned that he was also a closet alcoholic, when trouble began between the two men. They shared a kitchen with a third party.

The caretaker began to receive complaints that Tommy was not cleaning up after himself in the kitchen, and was stealing food from the alcoholic. We asked Tommy to stop taking the other person's food. The problems then went underground. Brad became angry one night when he was drinking. He began pounding on the wall of Tommy's bedroom, frightening the old man till he was afraid to even sit at the kitchen table to eat. Warnings that this unsuitable behavior would have to stop were given to Brad. Then Tommy began to try to get even. He began to miss the toilet of their shared bathroom. This irritated the third tenant who requested to be moved to another floor, and infuriated Brad. Brad would retaliate with wall pounding and complaints to the caretaker and phone calls to me. Both of the men were spoken to. The social worker was contacted too. A letter threatening eviction for continuance of his bad behavior was finally given to Brad, who by now had been a resident for six years. Then things seemed to calm down a bit, for a while.

One day I received a complaint that there was a dreadful odor coming from Tommy's room. With the proper notice I entered his room and cringed to find old decomposing food lying around on dirty plates, half eaten hamburgers under the bed, food scraps on the carpet, dishes filled with scummy water and cutlery on the shelves. Heaps of clothes were everywhere. The mattress had been ruined. The carpet was incredibly filthy and really needed to be replaced but I knew it would be useless unless the old man moved out. Egad! Even spiders were discovered nesting in huge cobwebs in one corner of his room.

I notified Tommy's social worker and immediately had the room and carpet cleaned. A new mattress and bedding were provided. A cleaner was hired to take care of Tommy's room every two weeks. He was charged with the cost of the cleanup while I paid for the new bed and bedding which had not been new when he moved in. Because I was already subsidizing him and another senior so that they could afford their rent, I only added a small amount to his rent each month to begin to collect the clean up expenses over time.

It became apparent that the man had become unable to care for himself. Letters were sent to his social worker and assisted living requesting help to find him a new home. I tried to get him relocated to no avail. Eventually at least regular once a day home care visits began.

A year went by before other complaints said that he was now missing the toilet again. Home Care then provided a commode for his room and began to provide twice daily services. The sweet old man refused to move to an assisted living care center. I felt helpless. I was powerless to have him removed. Only months later, through the help of a friend of his, he was eventually persuaded to move into a space in an assisted living building.

The caretaker discovered that Brad had been storing old bottles to be recycled behind the furnace in plastic bags. A total no no.

Then mould problems began. Mould was starting to be evident around the two second floor bathroom tiles and also began to show up on the bathroom ceilings in discolored patches. My handyman had to totally strip out the drywall, replace one shower stall and remodel two of the bathrooms because of the damp conditions. The tenants would not turn on the overhead fan, and indeed one would let the hot water run until it turned the bathroom into a steam room. I had to warn him that any further damage could be charged to him.

When damp was discovered in the corner of one lower room, I found out that water would seep into the basement level if there were heavy rains in the spring. I had to have remedial work completed to raise soil levels around the building. This area was then covered with large paving stones to aid the drainage away from the building. Downspouts were also extended to redirect the roof runoff. The damaged wall board was replaced with a waterproof type before repainting the corner in the affected room. All this while I paid for the tenant to live in a nearby motel!

After a few years, as the rental market tightened, the government changed the rental tenancy law. They limited rent increases to only once annually, just as I was about to give my six month rent increase notices to cover my escalating utility and property tax costs. I couldn't put through my anticipated increase until the following year. This put my rents below market rate.

The worst incident experienced was with one nice appearing well spoken young man, I will call Sam. He had come with his father to rent a room when my caretaker was in a hurry to rent before leaving for her holiday. He had seemed a very pleasant young man that was moving out of his parents' home, the caretaker was told. The proper checks were not completed before he received his room key. Unknowingly the caretaker had rented to a drug addict who smoked dope in his room.

Sam's unsavory friends began to visit at night, frightening some tenants. Sam began begging, threatening, and actually coercing other tenants for money. One sweet deaf young man in the room next to his was forced to give the addict his rent money, we learned. Sam used it to pay his rent but the deaf youth was not able to pay his own rent. On the third day after rent was late we always gave out an eviction notice. The deaf youth had to borrow money from his mother or he would be evicted. His mother alerted the caretaker and me about what had happened, but we didn't have sufficient grounds to evict Sam yet. Now the caretaker was getting worried and afraid. She alerted the Police, but there was nothing they could do.

When we luckily discovered that Sam, the addict, had removed his smoke detector from the ceiling I finally did have sufficient grounds to evict him on short notice for endangering the safety of other residents. In order to get rid of him I agreed to return his security deposit if he left his room clean. Sam desperately needed the money to get another place to live, and thus agreed and moved out. We heaved sighs of relief. He had only been living there for several months and did leave the room relatively clean.

When Sam left I took this opportunity to have a single master key made to open all of the rooms. All exterior doors were also rekeyed with copies given to the residents. We didn't want to have the addict or his unsavory friends return looking for ways to get money. As his former room was cleaned and prepared for re-renting, the caretaker discovered that Sam had carved a hole into the side of his mattress facing the wall. This was to hide his stash beneath the mattress cover. Replacement mattresses cost money. It was just one more costly surprise while running a rooming house.

THE FINAL STRAW

Then the day came when four departments from the city began a safe housing inspection. After inspecting every room and area, each department provided a letter with instructions for repairs. They required many changes but were willing to give the house development approval to continue to operate if these were completed. Lower income housing was sorely needed in the city. The inspectors required that all work be completed within a three month period. The requests from the first departments had seemed doable but when the last report from the Fire Department was finally clarified with all their changes I was upset and beside myself. How in heaven's name could I get all the work done in three months, let alone dip into my savings to pay for them. I wanted to cooperate and began to try to comply but their required changes began to add up to big dollars.

The Fire Department required a wired in fire alarm system complete with enunciator box. It seemed excessive since the building was just a raised two story house. But the Fire Department considered each room to be a separate suite with potential for cooking in the room. However, they really were only sleeping rooms with all cooking done in the kitchens. Wired in heat detectors were required to be added in every room in addition to the smoke detectors already in place in each. To meet the Fire Department's approval this had to be designed by an engineer. I groaned. More money to be spent I thought as I heaved a big sigh. All the bedroom doors were to be changed to fire rated doors. All the hallway lengths were to be shortened to not over fifteen feet in length which meant the addition of walls and doors part way down the halls. Fire rated drywall and a sprinkler system were required to be added to the furnace room. Each kitchen was to be enclosed with additional walls and fire proof doors. Thank goodness they didn't require a whole new exit and external stair system, since the window openings were large enough to provide an escape.

The Health Department required either new windows or that the double sliding aluminum windows be re-weather stripped and painted between the panes. They saw a puddle of water near the laundry equipment that was to be investigated.

The Electrical Department required pruning of an apple tree that was too close to the incoming power lead. They also spotted a breaker that required rewiring.

The Safety Department required that the older style wrought iron railings at the front entry be changed to increase their height four more inches to meet newer building standards. A small foundation crack was to be repaired.

The costs of these and other requested changes added up to at least $30,000.00. So much for my good cash flow I thought. This was the final straw. My caretaker wanted to leave too. After nine years both of us had had enough. Giving a $30,000.00 discount for the safe housing restoration costs to the purchasers, I quickly sold the building and breathed a sigh of relief.

The government and I both made a considerable amount of money by the sale of the rooming house which had gone up over three and a quarter times in value since I purchased it. Now I had an opportunity to find other investments.

"Rich people use every dollar as a "seed" that can be planted to earn a hundred more dollars, which can then be replanted to earn a thousand more dollars."

T. Harv Eker

TIPS & EXPENSIVE LESSONS

1. While the cash flow generated by a rooming house is good, the headaches are many. We had 69 people move in and out in nine years but seldom had any vacancies.

2. Use a Realtor for your purchase who is thorough and is familiar with rooming house requirements.

3. Before finalizing your purchase get a price for insurance. Rooming houses have a high loss history as a group and the premiums can be very much higher than you might expect.

4. Ensure you receive all the pertinent information regarding zoning, city development approvals, easements or charges on the title, any encroachments, any environmental assessments and real property report. Or scout it out yourself thoroughly before committing to your purchase. Allow enough time in your purchase agreement condition clause to research everything well before removing your conditions.

5. Make certain by contacting the city that the building use complies with development permits and zoning.

6. Find out if there are any outstanding safe housing orders or Fire Department requirements.

7. Get an up to date real property report showing fence lines, etc. to ensure there are no building or land encroachments.

8. Pay for a proper building inspection before committing to your purchase. If it discloses problems get the vendor to pay or share the cost to remedy.

9. Use a mortgage broker if necessary to obtain financing. My broker found me financing in another province when the local banks would not lend money on a rooming house.

10. If there are vacancies leave them vacant so that you can put in your own thoroughly researched tenants. If landlord and tenant laws in your jurisdiction allow, you may wish to request vacant possession when you purchase in order to place your own people.

11. Take an inventory of all furnishings. Keep this up to date after you take possession since tenants will swap things between their rooms on occasion without telling you.

12. Have a special master key system installed by a locksmith.

13. Who will be your onsite caretaker? Without a good honest caretaker there will be many more problems. He or she will need to be a people person with no race prejudices.

14. Will your caretaker do all the cleaning or will you also need to hire a cleaner?

15. Will the caretaker do your banking?

16. Make certain your telephone lines that tenants have access to are toll restricted.

17. Teach your caretaker the rental procedures that you wish to have followed. Set up a key safety system. Provide them with duplicate bank deposit forms, duplicate receipt books and all the necessary tenant application and leasing forms. These include applications to rent, smoke detector acknowledgment forms, rules of occupancy to sign, duplicate leases, blank preprinted 14 day eviction notices, triplicate condition inspection forms, cleaning requirements to receive return of security deposit, inventory of furnishing acceptance forms, blank notices for room entry, and security deposit settlement forms.

18. Always collect the security deposit equal to one month's rent in cash or a money order made out to you. Take part of it to hold the room until you can check the tenant suitability. Refund it if necessary.

19. Once a tenant is in place it can be very hard to remove him or her. Do as much checking as possible with previous landlords. Check references. Do a credit check before accepting a tenant.

20. Study the Residential Tenancies or Landlord & Tenant Act so that you know your rights and remedies available.

21. Get all tenants to sign that they acknowledge the smoke detector is in working order. Have them sign a statement to accept your rules and that they will abide by them. Act immediately to maintain your house rules. If an eviction notice is warranted act promptly.

22. Do not let unpaid rent situations get out of hand. If rent has not been paid by the third day have your caretaker issue an eviction order. Put in a clause that it can be rescinded provided rent is paid within fifteen days. If they don't pay then the timing of this eviction gives you a few days to clean and re-rent without losing the following month's rent.

23. While being fair and reasonable, don't be afraid to raise your rents as often as you are legally allowed in order to keep up with the market. Your eventual selling price will be largely based on your revenue.

24. Provide correct notices before entering tenant's rooms except in an emergency.

25. People will do what people do. They won't always follow your rules. Nor will they wipe their feet so you will have to clean the carpets often.

26. Free laundry equipment can prevent loss of your revenue through break-ins and theft. Consider using only prepaid cards in place of coins if you have a coin operated laundry.

27. You may need to store certain possessions left behind by tenants for the time required by law. Save some storage space for this in the garage.

28. Plan on having more repairs and more cleaning expenses than normal.

29. Accept that the steam and damp from many showers will take their toll on your bathroom finishes. Your carpets will need extra cleaning, since tenants seldom take off their dirty footwear at the door. Build in a reserve for extra repair funds.

In Chapter 9 motel ownership and rental pools are highlighted.

Rental forms follow:

XXX Ave & XXX Street

CASH FLOW ANALYSIS

2 ½ storey 14 room Rooming House with Garage

Approximate Purchase Price	**210,000.00**

Financial / Refinancing

Current First Mortgage	119,100.00
Equity approx. (43.1%)	90,900.00

Pro-forma Income	**Monthly**	**Annual**
Market Rent	2,845.00	34,140.00
Vacancy (estimated @ 1%)	30.00	360.00
Current Income	**2,815.00**	**33,780.00**

Expenses

Property Taxes 20____	(187.65)	(2,251.79)
Utilities gas/water/sewer/waste/cable/telephone	(559.85)	(6,718.20)
Property Management	0.00	0.00
Insurance	(166.67)	(2,000.00)
Resident Manager leasing (Free suite rent is not included in income)	(50.00)	(600.00)
Repairs and Maintenance	(50.00)	(600.00)
Total Expenses	**1,014.17**	**12,169.99**
Cash Flow Before Debt Payment	**1,800.83**	**21,610.01**
First Mortgage Payment (6.7% 5 year closed – term end Aug 1, 2004)	(862.32)	(10,347.84)
Cash Flow	938.51	11,262.17
First Mortgage Principal Reduction	197.00	2,364.00
NET RETURN	**1,135.51**	**14,761.68**

Sample Rental Expense and Revenue for Rooming house.

Advertising	$	-
Insurance	$	-
Mortgage expense	$	-
Maintenance /Repairs	$	-
Appliance repair	$	-
Building Repairs	$	-
Lock & key	$	-
Furnishings,	$	-
Appliance & equipment	$	-
Cleaning supplies & bedding	$	-
Carpet cleaning	$	-
Carpet replacement	$	-
Janitor Cleaning	$	-
Room Cleaning	$	-
Property tax	$	-
Management & administration fees	$	-
Leasing fees	$	-
Caretaker wage (includes free suite rent)	$	-
Salaries, wages and benefits	$	-
Utilities/Water/Sewer/Drainage/Waste	$	-
Electricity/ Gas	$	-
Other expenses	$	-
Telephone	$	-
Cable TV	$	-
Bad debt	$	-
Total Expense	**$**	**-**
Revenue		
Rent	$	-
Cleaning recovery	$	-
Security deposit forfeiture	$	-
Penalties	$	-
Revenue	**$**	**-**
Net Revenue	**$**	**-**

Condition Report for _____ Room # _____

I _____, acknowledge receipt of the following furnishings and agree to leave them in good condition, except for normal wear and tear, when I vacate my room. Any damage or problems with the room have been listed below.

Move- in Move-out

_____Bed base

_____Box spring   .

_____Bed skirt

_____Mattress_____size

_____Blanket_____color

_____One pair of sheets

_____One night table

_____One chest of drawers

_____Two side chairs

_____One easy chair_____color

Move-in Move-out

_____One table with _____top

_____Pillow(s)

_____Pillow cases

_____One refrigerator

_____Venetian blinds

_____Comforter_____ color

_____ Window screen

_____ Table Lamp with _ shade

_____ Floor lamp_____ color

_____Telephone_____ color

Other (please identify and list)

_____

_____

_____

Other problems with walls, door, ceiling, ceiling light

_____

_____

_____

Inspections should be conducted when the premises are vacant unless the landlord and tenant or their agents otherwise agree. The

117

inspection of the premises was conducted on _____,20____
by _____ and by _____

I, _____, agree that this report fairly
represents the condition of the premises. I,
_____acknowledge receipt of one set of keys
consisting of one key for Room #_____, one key for side door____
one key for main floor / or lower _____which I agree to return when
I vacate the premises.

Dated at _____this _____ day of_____20____

_____   _____   _____
Witness   Tenant   Room #

Tenant acknowledges receipt of copy_____

Move- out inspection was conducted on

_____.20___ by

_____and _____

I,_____acknowledge that condition on move -

out is as listed above. _____   Tenant

signature

118

NOTICE OF EVICTION FOR NON-PAYMENT OF RENT

To_____Date_____

Room _____

You are notified that you owe rent in the amount of $
_____for the month of _____and late penalties of
$_____ per day that the rent is overdue.

If you do not pay this rent within 14 days your tenancy of Room #
_____ is hereby terminated effective at twelve o'clock PM on the 17th
day of _____ and you are required to vacate room # _____by
that time.

If you pay the overdue rent plus late charges in full prior to that date,
your tenancy will be reinstated. You must pay your rent in cash,
money order, or certified cheque.

If you have not paid the rent or moved within 15 days, a lawsuit will
be filed to evict you. If you pay your rent on or before the 15th day,
you may stay.

Signed,

_____

(Landlord) or (Landlord's agent)

This notice was:

_____ hand delivered in person to the tenant on the third day of

_____ posted on the door to Room #_____

Signed

_____

(Landlord's agent)

FOR THE RETURN OF SECURITY DEPOSIT
THE FOLLOWING REQUIREMENTS MUST BE COMPLETED.

1. Defrost and clean refrigerator and freezer. Unplug fridge and leave the door propped open.

2. Wash bedding.

3. Remove fingerprints and marks from walls, doors, and furniture.

4. Wash ceiling light fixture, and dust lamps and shade(s).

5. Vacuum, and if soiled, spot clean or shampoo the carpet in your room.

6. Wipe windows clean.

7. Remove all of your food from the common kitchen and personal articles from the bathroom(s).

8. Remove any garbage.

Any cleaning deemed necessary in the sole opinion of the landlord, or caretaker, will be deducted from the security deposit. Any damage done to furnishings, bedding, blinds, carpets, etc. beyond that which is deemed to be normal wear and tear will be deducted from the security deposit.

SATISFACTORY INSPECTION OF YOUR ROOM BY THE LANDLORD IS ABSOLUTELY NECESSARY. THANK YOU

GARAGE STORAGE AGREEMENT

This agreement is made on the _____day of_____20___ , between

The landlord: and   The tenant:

_____   _____
_____   _____

Phone _____ Fax _____

The landlord agrees to rent to the tenant a portion of storage space in the garage at _____ _____for the purpose of storing household possessions.

The term of tenancy shall be for _____
beginning _____20__ And ending on the _____day of _____, 20__ or be for a monthly term beginning on the _____day of _____, 20__ and continuing monthly periodic until the Landlord or the Tenant ends the tenancy in the manner required under the Residential Tenancies Act and its regulations. The landlord and the tenant must give written notice.

The rent is : $_____

Other _____ $_____

Total monthly rent: $_____

Rent includes the use of _____% of the floor space and vertical air space above it or _____ square feet of storage space, namely _____feet by _____feet of floor space and the air space above it. The tenant will pay the total rent on the First day of each month starting on the _____day of _____20____

Conditions of rental

Rent checks are to be made in the name of the Landlord (above) and delivered to _____or to the Landlord at the Landlord's address above.

The Landlord agrees to supply electricity for lighting use only.

The Landlord will advise the Tenant of any change in ownership of the premises within seven days of that change. In the event of a change of ownership the Tenant will be given 90 days notice to remove his /her goods from the garage premises.

The Tenant must not store any combustible material or flammable liquid on the property premises or inside the garage.

The Tenant must not store articles owned by other persons in their portion of the garage storage space.

The Landlord may request a security deposit of $_____ from which the Landlord may make deductions for any clean-up required as a result of the use of the storage area by the Tenant and the repair of damage to the premises caused or permitted by the Tenant.

The Landlord **will not be held liable for any loss or damage** to the Tenants goods while they are stored on the Landlord's premises. The Tenant must insure his or her own property against damage or loss. The Landlord's insurance coverage **does not provide any protection** to the Tenant for the Tenant's benefit in the event the stored goods are lost or stolen while stored at the premises.

I/We _____hereby acknowledge that the Landlord and others will also be using portions of the garage premises for their storage and will have access to the garage without the direct supervision of the caretaker or the Landlord.

I/We _____ hereby acknowledge and accept the conditions described above for the storage of our personal articles in the garage
at_____ Dated at _____ this ____
date of _____, 20___

Tenant(s)_____Tenant(s)_____

Landlord_____ (Or landlord's agent)

The Tenant hereby acknowledges receipt of a copy of this agreement._____

SECURITY DEPOSIT STATEMENT

DATE:_____REGARDING:_____

TENANT_____   DEPOSIT: $_____

_____   INTEREST: $_____

_____   TOTAL: $_____

DEDUCTIONS:

_____ $_____

_____ $_____

_____ $_____

_____ $_____

_____ $_____

_____ $_____

_____ $_____

_____ $_____

_____ $_____

TOTAL DEDUCTIONS: $_____ $_____

BALANCE TO TENANT or

ACCOUNTS PAYABLE

$_____

_____

COMMENTS:

AUTHORIZED SIGNATURE: _____ DATE:_____

Please sign and return this portion of the Statement. Thank you.

I,_____ hereby acknowledge receipt of the
sum of $_____as full and final settlement of this matter.

Signature:_____ Date: _____

CHAPTER 9

MOTELS MAKE MONEY?

RENTAL POOLS ARE TROUBLE FREE?

More mistakes and lesson tips

MOTELS MAKE MONEY?

*"Working hard for money is an old formula born in the
day of cave men."*

Robert T. Kiyosaki

After the apartment building sale fiasco (discussed in chapter 7) we purchased a 38-room motel in Calgary. It was on the highway from Banff. We selected it because it was on a main traffic inlet from the mountains. There was a good Restaurant within a block, a service station and grocery store close by. It seemed ideal in many ways. It was an older two story style in the shape of a T. Clad in red brick it looked inviting and in good condition outside. The parking area was paved and adequate. There was a small resident manager suite next to the office in the central wing. The double and twin bedded motel rooms, all with baths were simple but a reasonable size. They were very bare and tired looking, however. One larger room was a blah looking honeymoon suite. There were no pictures on any of the walls and all the rooms were in need of new bedspreads and some color to enliven them.

We purchased in March in order to take advantage of the summer tourist season. A number of the rooms had already been rented at lower rates to longer term people in the off seasons. These folk were starting to move out since their off season rates were expiring.

We located a good experienced older couple to manage for us. They ordered cleaning supplies and oversaw the two maids who did the room cleaning. The manager also received the revenue from the pop machine that he installed right away.

My husband had triplicate room rental slips printed so that we would have an audit trail of the room rentals for accounting. We soon discovered that the government tourist department also required detailed reports of room rentals every month. These were to be submitted to them each month.   The tourist department paid no remuneration for our preparation time.

Photos were taken for making advertising postcards. I handled the payroll and did the books under the direction of my accountant husband. I had no experience in bookkeeping. The frustration of trying to teach me book keeping soon became a marriage problem, but we soldiered on.

In order to attract a better clientele, the rooms needed cleaning and dressing up. New bedspreads were ordered from a hotel supply company. To save cost a variety of small cloth picture panels were purchased and then stretched and glued over foam board to hang on the walls. They looked great and if they were stolen the loss would be minimal.

When our new manager moved in he decided that the rental office was too big with its wasted lounge area. His apartment was too small and he wanted a bath tub instead of the shower stall that was there. So we allowed him to take space from the office to enlarge his apartment and add the tub. The good thing about it was that it likely made the motel more saleable later.

Meanwhile we fell into a routine. When the manager was on his weekends off, my husband or I would man the rental office and direct the maids. Both of us were also working weekdays at other jobs as well. Now I am a morning person and was normally up by 6:00 am. I had a difficult time staying awake until 2:00 am in the hope of renting the last spaces. Some nights I gave up earlier in exhaustion and put on the no vacancy sign early. We hadn't realized how tiring the experience would be when long weekend hours were added to our other employment hours.

Sometimes the maids were sick or did not show up and we had to help clean the rooms and change the beds. We discovered that dependable staff is a must but not always easy to find.

We began to learn some of the renter's tricks. For instance people with dogs would register saying they did not have a dog. They would keep their pet hidden in their vehicle to avoid the extra pet fee.

A single man would rent a room and then out of the side window we would glimpse his two buddies moving in with him as well for free. Drunks would overstay their check out time and have to be roused.

We would have to try to control noisy parties. Following noisy parties or sick drunks extra cleanups would be needed. It many respects running a motel provided an interesting education into human behavior.

We had a plumber look at the boiler system when we realized there was a heating problem. He told us that when the motel was built the heating system and water lines had been installed with previously used materials. The plumber told us that even the radiators in each room had been installed with recycled parts. We surmised the developer must have run out of money when he was building the place.

When summer came we began to realize why the previous owner had sold the motel in early spring. There was no air conditioning in the rooms. The rooms were too hot. The fire wall requirements did not allow wall openings for air conditioning units to be placed on the rear wall of the building. Since the walls were cinder block filled with sand then covered with red brick, it was going to be expensive to put in individual air conditioning. The brick facing under each front window would have to be opened up instead to fit in an air conditioner.

If we were going to air condition the rooms we would want the words "air conditioned" added to our sign. I began looking into the cost with the neon sign company. It was expensive but if we signed a long term contract they would build the cost into our monthly sign rental payments.

Then the city road department sent a letter to advise that they would begin doing sewer line maintenance and road allowance changes along our street. This would restrict easy access to the motel for a lengthy period of time. With limited access, potential tenants would likely just drive on by. The previous owner likely knew about it prior to putting the motel up for sale. We discovered we had no say in the circumstances. Registered on our title was a right of way agreement that spelled out the city's authority to do road work without compensating us for lost business. No wonder the vendor had sold the business.

About this time we began to realize that even when it was full the motel was not making enough money. Even with us working weekends our overhead was too costly. The motel was too small to support a manager as well as to provide us with profit. Before eight months were out we realized we had to sell.

Friends used our example as a basis for making a motel purchase, and bought a larger motel with a restaurant. It was located in a small northern town close to an Indian reserve. They had great occupancy with good income from oil field worker renters employed in the area.

However, they soon discovered that there was a limited mostly native employment pool to draw from. There was such a small pool of dependable employees to hire, that our friends often found themselves being chef, waiter, and dish washer as well as managers and cleaners. They were up nights and weekends on top of everything else.

They soon discovered that when they fired a person for non-performance, they would in desperation have no alternative but to hire them back again later. Due to the labor shortage the fired staff would be snapped up by a rival motel who would also later fire them. Thus the motels and restaurants would bounce staff between them. Our friends stuck it out for several years, until they finally became too exhausted and sold their motel.

> *"This is only a game. Sometimes you win and sometimes you learn."*
>
> Robert T. Kiyosaki

TIPS & EXPENSIVE LESSONS

1. Thirty eight rooms to rent was not sufficient to afford a live in manager. By my husband's calculations, if there was a mortgage a motel needed at least 60 rooms in order to pay an onsite manager wages as well as provide any kind of return on the investment. Anything smaller would require the owner to live in and be his own manager.

2. Selecting a great rental location is only part of the necessary due diligence.

3. What easements or agreements are registered on the title?

4. What street improvement has the city planned for the coming years? Is there a master plan for any improvements for the area?

5. What do you know about motel management? Who will teach you?

6. Are you a people person?

7. How are you at staff hiring and management?

8. How do you plan to man the motel? Who will manage it while your manager is on vacation?

9. Who will handle pay roll and accounting records?

10. What government departments will require reports from you?

11. Detailed inspection of the mechanical systems as well as each of the rooms is necessary.

12. Check how well the sink drains and toilets are functioning.

13. If the planned purchase has appliances in the suites what condition are they in?

14. Examine the books of the vendor to determine what the occupancy percentages are.

15. Is there a master key system in place? How are keys controlled?

16. If you will be located in a small town can you obtain the necessary staff?

17. If the motel comes with a restaurant will the restaurant pay for itself? Can you lease it out for another to run? If so how dependable are they?

18. As owners how will your motel revenue be affected if the restaurant has inconsiderate staff or serves poor meals? How would a bad reputation affect your revenue? Could you make money if the restaurant is permanently closed?

19. Not having air conditioning definitely means fewer rentals in warm weather.

20. Is there a swimming pool? Is there a contract for its maintenance? Health rules will require regular water tests and specific cleaning methods.

RENTAL POOLS ARE TROUBLE FREE?

This type of investment in real estate can be relatively trouble free. Someone else takes on the landlording headaches. You along with other investors each buy one or more units in a condominium apartment complex. A property manager looks after the property for you and sends you a net payment each month based on the net return of the building. The manager will deduct for all expenses. These may include utilities, property taxes, condominium fees, administration, management, onsite caretaker, janitor, and repairs. All owners in the pool will share in the vacancy loss based on their unit factor share in the property. In addition to a management agreement for the condominium there will be a separate agreement for the rental pool. You will have fees for both deducted from your revenue by the manager.

I became an owner of several units in a large rental pool in another city I never saw the project except in photographs since it was out of town about 500 miles away. While in the end I did make a profit the experience came along with a few headaches.

I relied on the proforma information given to me at the presentation meeting. It indicated that I would have a positive cash flow. The salesman giving the talk indicated that the units were undervalued about $15,000.00 when compared with others across the street. It seemed that everyone was lining up to make a purchase so I joined them. I knew very little about the property.

The developer had purchased an old run down rental site of 320 units to convert into condominiums. It was located in a great rental area, but was already close to thirty years old. The developer restored the property to a degree before commencing his rental pool sales. The pictures I was shown looked attractive with grown trees and lawns. The developer was putting in several more million dollars in upgrades and the retrofitting of the recreation center. Each suite was being renewed with new appliances, carpet, linoleum and paint. No restoration maintenance would be required for a few years I thought. Another chunk of money was also placed in the reserve fund, so it seemed at the time to be a good deal.

However I hadn't realized the magnitude of the regular maintenance and staffing that would be required for such a site. There were nine blocks of buildings each with a boiler to maintain. From the pictures I had seen I thought there were only three buildings. Nine boilers to keep running cost money.

Because I was purchasing rental property I had to put down 35% of the purchase price for each suite and be approved for the mortgages. I didn't have enough available financing for the down payment on two units. The excellent broker I was directed to found a smaller bank in another province that provided me with a $15,000.00 line of credit without any security. This enabled me to make up the shortfall. Because I had an excellent credit rating I was not even required to provide any personal guarantees.

It soon became apparent that considering the age, condition of the property and its shear size, the reserves were inadequate. For nine buildings connected to a large underground parkade with a park on its roof there would be nowhere near enough money to cover expenses over the years.

The developer's refurbishing of the suites and the buildings took several years to complete, since labor was hard to get at that time. My suites were not refurbished until a year after I had purchased.

The buildings began to require expensive maintenance. The siding on the buildings was brown cedar wood which required painting every few years. Nine boilers needed maintenance. Both the rental office and a recreation center required staffing. An indoor swimming pool required cleaning and maintenance. Insufficient site parkade parking spaces meant that vehicles plugged the sides of the narrow internal roadways, causing tenant problems.

The property values were not as high as the salesperson had suggested they were in the beginning. For the first several years there was little appreciation in value. The revenue was just barely enough to cover my mortgages and line of credit.

Then the first special assessment was levied. The Fire Department required new fire alarm systems be added to the buildings. Now I had to subsidize the units until my share of the assessment was paid.

THE FIRE

Then in November I read in the newspaper that one of the nine blocks of units had had a major fire. All units were evacuated safely. Luckily the staff and the community were able to provide all of the tenants with other places to stay since the weather was now very cold. Even though a portion of the building was still standing, the complete building needed to be rebuilt. One of my units was in that building. Thank goodness for insurance I thought.

The rental pool had good insurance coverage that provided for loss of rent. The rental pool began to receive these compensation funds so my share of rent returns did not go down.

But then in the spring when contractors were being readied to begin rebuilding it was discovered that a number of areas had evidence of mould. Under the terms of the insurance policy this would nullify the complete insurance coverage unless it could be proven that the mould had occurred as a result of the fire fighting. Perhaps pouring water on to quench the fire had allowed mould to develop, we argued. All rebuilding had to stop until inspectors could make a determination and an agreement could be reached with the insurers. Luckily for us, the mould issue was at last set aside in our favor and rebuilding could commence.

But now more than a year had elapsed ending the one year coverage for compensation of lost rent. The units were not yet ready for occupancy, indeed it was almost six more months until occupancy permits were finally issued by the city. Down went our revenue and down went my monthly income share. I decided to sell one apartment not realizing much gain but enough to cover realty fees and all my expenses.

Then boom times came to the community. After a few more years the rents climbed high and property values increased. With increased mortgage financing I was able to take out more than my original equity to invest elsewhere. I was shocked, however, at how much the manager was now being paid. I felt it was an excessive fee for the duties they performed. The management company had negotiated their management fee based on a percentage of rent revenue. There was no cap on this. As rents escalated so did their share even though the services they provided did not change.

I held on for several years while the values climbed but chose to sell when it became apparent that the reserve fund was totally inadequate. Major balcony replacements for rotted wood had become necessary at a price of $3,500 to $12,000 each for the worst balconies. Multiply that by three hundred and twenty units and the reserve fund of over a million dollars would be wiped out completely and then some. Had I continued as an owner I likely would have received a very large special assessment to pay for my share of the necessary work. It was definitely time to sell.

NOT SO EASY TO SELL

Using a local Realtor I had never met I put the remaining unit on the market. The manager's onsite staff would not allow my Realtor in to see the unit. They said she had to get a written authority from their head office in another city . There was a lengthy delay until this hurdle was overcome. I also provided a notice authorizing my Realtor to act on my behalf in regard to arranging showings. I sent my written notice to the management company head office. I advised that I was putting the unit on the market and to give the month by month tenant the required ninety day notice when I notified them that the unit had been sold. The onsite managers said that their policy was that I would have to provide the notice to vacate to the tenants myself. They would not do it.

I was angry, and managed to get hold of the head office manager and pointed out in no uncertain terms that there was no way I could give the tenants notice since I was not a signatory to the lease agreement, nor had I ever been given their names. I reminded the managers that they provided and executed the lease agreements and they would have to be the ones to notify their tenants. The manager backed down and grudgingly agreed to provide the notice when I had a sale for the unit.

My Realtor was finally able to connect with the tenants to see the condition of the unit. She told me that the place was in general disorder. It was full of empty bottles, garbage bags and clothing lying about and would not show well. She was able to appeal to the tenants to get rid of the garbage and was finally able to show it to prospective tenants.

I conditionally sold the apartment and advised the management company by fax to please give the tenants their notice before the end of June. Possession date was set for October the 1st, in accordance with the ninety day notice period. I also asked the Realtor to advise the tenants that the unit had been sold and to give the tenants a copy of the notice to vacate that I had prepared. The realtor taped the notice on the unit's door in accordance with the tenancy law since the tenants were not home at the time of her visit.

The purchaser was preapproved for financing and shortly all sales conditions were removed. However the final date of removal of the sale conditions fell on July 7th, about a week after the start of the ninety day notice period began. The tenants were advised that the unit was now sold. One of the tenants stormed into the onsite office. He advised the clerk that they had not received proper notice and would not be moving. The tenant said he knew their rights and that under the law they could not legally be given notice until the sale was complete. The tenant pointed out that a conditional sale was not legally considered a sale until all the conditions were removed. The rental market was very tight and he had no place they could move to, so would not move. A new ninety day notice would delay possession until November 1st since it could only be given at the end of a month.

My Realtor contacted the purchaser through their Realtor and asked if they would extend the possession date. They refused. They had sold their property and would have no where to go if the possession date was extended. In hurried conferences with the Realtor and discussions with the onsite staff, I suggested that I would offer the tenants a cash incentive if they would move out early.

Luckily for me a vacancy became available in the complex. The tenant did finally, with persuasion from the site staff, agree to move early. The staff warned him that they had already taken a deposit from people on a waiting list for that suite but they would instead provide it to him if he would move early. The deciding clincher was that they did not know when they might have another vacancy in such tight market conditions.

When possession finally occurred, after a further delay so that the carpets could be cleaned, this sale made me an excellent profit even after the tax department took its large bite.

CAUTIONS:

Suites in existing rental pool buildings often sell at lower prices. This is because of a perception that many landlord groups do not keep up their properties in the same way that owner occupiers do. Buyers who plan to occupy their suites expect that they will be surrounded by uncaring tenants instead of other owners. They also anticipate that the rental pool owners will only spend the minimum on upkeep of the property.

If entering into a rental pool agreement, consider these items:

1. Do your due diligence on the developer.

2.   Do not believe the sales pitch without checking into the details yourself.

3.   What is the history and track record of the developer?

4.   How will the developer meet his financial commitments to refurbish the property?

5.   Does the proforma revenue valuation seem adequate?

6.   Read the rental pool agreement. Who will be responsible to pay for appliance or carpet replacement and regular maintenance repairs within your unit?

7.   Read the rental pool management agreement. How is the manager to be paid? Will it be a commission based on rent revenue? If rents climb a lot is there a cap on this?

8.   Read the rental pool insurance policy or at least a summary. Does it protect you against loss of rental income? What are the exclusions? Mould is excluded in most policies now. There will also be a separate condominium policy.

9.   What are the insurance deductibles? Who is responsible to pay deductibles if a loss affects your suite? As an owner you may wish to have landlord protective coverage as well.

10. Review the rental pool budget as well as the condominium budget. Both the rental pool and the condominium will assess costs for management and repairs each in their own area. The rental pool for suite interiors and leasing or rental staff and the condominium for management of the exteriors and certain utility expenses. Your net revenue will be the remainder after both deductions.

11. Read the condominium bylaws and policies if any. Their enforceable wording may prevent renting to other than family members, or people with pets for instance. They may contain fining provisions that could affect you.

12. Has a reserve study been completed? Is it current? Is there a reserve funding plan available? Condominium reserve studies are required to be completed every five years in some jurisdictions. They provide a yearly expenditure estimate of the funds that will be necessary to pay for the repairs and replacements of the common property elements and structures. They project for periods of 25 years indicating the likely life span of a building item that will require replacement at some time in the future.

13. How adequate are the present reserves for capital replacements? If in your estimation the reserves are under-funded you will need to have your own savings fund available for the eventual special assessment.

14. Are any major repairs looming that the developer will not be completing? What is the age and condition of expensive items such as the roof or windows?

15. How well is the building constructed? Any signs of settlement cracks?

16. Are the exterior finishes low maintenance?

17. What state of repair is the building in for its age?

18. Are the fire systems current to the building code?

19. Is there adequate parking? Is there visitor parking?

20. Are their recreational facilities included? These can add considerably to expenses. If there is an indoor year round swimming pool this can cost approximately $30,000.00 per year or more in water, chemicals, testing, cleaning and maintenance alone. Each apartment in a seventy unit building with a pool will pay approximately $35.00 per month in extra fees. The extra rental value to you may be negligible.

21. Is the building located in an area that is easy to rent for good fees? Is it served by nearby transit?

22. Is there a positive cash flow after you pay for financing? If not, how much will you need to subsidize it each month?

23. If the condominium fees go up or a special assessment is required will you have enough cash flow or a savings fund to cover the expense? The risk of special assessments is very high if the reserve fund balance is too low when compared to the reserve study and plan.

24. How good is the reputation of the rental pool management company? Can you obtain references?

25. Is there an onsite resident rental manager?

26. How do they screen the new tenants before renting to them? Well screened tenants mean less damage and fewer vacancies.

27. Is the condominium managed by a separate company or also by the rental pool company?

28. Do they administer in accordance with the condominium bylaws?

29. When you come to sell make certain that you are familiar with the tenant notice requirements spelled out in residency law for your area.

30. When a unit is a rental unit it is easiest to sell when your unit has been vacated. Some tenants are not cooperative and can prevent or obstruct your sale by their untidiness making the property look less desirable. The difficulty is that you could have it sitting vacant for a long time if you do not find a buyer right away.

31. Suites in existing rental pool buildings often sell at lower prices. This is because of a perception that many landlord groups do not keep up their properties in the same way that owner occupiers do. Buyers who plan to occupy their suites expect that they will be surrounded by uncaring tenants instead of other owners. They also anticipate that the rental pool owners will only spend the minimum on upkeep of the property

Owning an illegal fourplex with attendant noise problems is covered in Chapter 10.

CHAPTER 10

HEADACHES OF A SIDE BY SIDE DUPLEX WITH SUITES

Illegal suites; Extra cost refinancing; Unshared maintenance expense; Unending noise & tenant Problems; Incompatible tenants; Failed eviction; A hurried rental mistake; Derelict pickup truck; Calling it quits; Telephone questions; Advertising; Buying, showing & and renting tips; Rental forms

"It is easier to stay out of trouble than it is to get out of trouble"
Warren Buffett

HEADACHES OF A SIDE BY SIDE DUPLEX WITH SUITES

Each type of property has its own set of problems. I didn't have a clue about what I was up against before buying. If my story saves you from going through even one of these incidents then the telling of it is of value.

Another purchase I made was an older duplex building. Shortly after it was built, the town it was located in was annexed by the city. The street was quiet and in a good rental area, or so I thought. A large tree in the center of the front yard made the property look appealing. The roof was recent; the walls were stucco. Each 1080 square foot side had a two bedroom one bathroom suite upstairs with a finished two bedroom suite in the raised bilevel basement. Each of the four suites had its own laundry machines. The two separate yards were fenced each with single garages and parking pads entered from the lane. There was a separate title and different lender financing for each side.

ILEGAL SUITES

Once again there were lessons to learn. The real property report indicated that the side yards were less than current bylaw requirements for the building to be a fourplex, but a permit had been given for duplex use. However the zoning class did include fourplexes, so I did nothing about it. Technically the fourplex use was illegal, but the good cash flow once again obscured my vision.

I suspected that the construction of the lower suites did not entirely meet the current building code. There was only one furnace on each side, instead of two. Head room in some portions of the basement suites was not the code required seven feet height. However the lower suites did have their own exterior entrances. The original access had been through an interior basement stairwell connected to the upper suite. That basement door between the upper and lower suites had been locked off from both sides. The windows downstairs were a good size; adequate for an emergency exit.

There was a beautiful large maple tree in the center of the two front yards. Before I purchased I checked with the city about the sewer lines that ran beneath the tree. My research showed quite a history of sewer back up call outs over the years.

THE PURCHASE

My estimates based on rents indicated the price requested was too high. I decided to make a considerably lower offer. I wanted to buy by assuming the first mortgages with a vendor take back and low down payment.

The vendor offered to hold a second mortgage on each side of the dwelling but he wanted a personal guarantee. I refused to provide it. He checked my credit history and finally relented. When I discovered the potential for sewer back up problems, I managed to get the vendor to execute a sewer line responsibility agreement. It would pay for any sewer back up damage and resulting repair that might occur for a two year period.

I inspected each suite and met the tenants. Their leases were reviewed. Once again I accepted existing tenants. A big mistake, but hard to avoid. Unless I planned to live in the unit where I wished to evict a tenant I could not legally remove them until the end of their lease. One lower suite was vacant. The vendor found a quiet older single man to rent it and he moved in shortly before I took possession.

The tenants in the upper suites paid the utilities and collected their share from the lower tenants.

EXTRA COST REFINANCING

I assumed both mortgages but they were at higher than current interest rates. On one side the previous owner had received a cash back payment of $4,000.00 when he took out his mortgage. I went to refinance nine months later with the same bank after rates had fallen. It was about a year and a half into a five year mortgage term. In order to do so I had to pay back to the bank a prorated share of the $4,000.00 cash back received by the previous owner. Often a bank will waive the standard three month penalty when a person refinances with the same bank. But not the recovery of a cash back deal, I sadly discovered. However, the bank allowed it to be paid by increasing the mortgage. Both sides were refinanced with a future sale in mind, since I did not know how long I might keep the building. Lower interest rates would make the financing more attractive to future purchasers.

UNSHARED MAINTENANCE PROBLEMS

One wooden side fence was rotten and a section fell out one day. The owner of the next door building was approached to share in the cost of our shared boundary fence. He refused. So my handyman replaced only the damaged section since I had to foot the total bill.

Washer and dryer maintenance was an ongoing problem. Each unit had its own laundry pair but the equipment was old. I located a good used appliance company to handle the replacements as necessary with reconditioned machines.

I wished I had done what Tim Johnston, formerly of R.E.I.N had recommended. When he bought a property he would give his first tenants the old laundry equipment and make them responsible for their own repairs. Then he would rent to future tenants without laundry equipment. However, having on site laundry equipment can be attractive to potential tenants.

A middle aged woman tenant I will name Katy, was supposed to do the yard work for her side of the duplex. When she didn't I resigned myself to hire a landscaper to clean up the weeds. When Katy's lease was due I sent her a letter that she could choose to care for the grounds or her renewal would be at a higher rent. She accepted the clause to care for the grounds at the lower rent and assured me that it would all be looked after.

What a lie. The weeds grew out between the patio stones in the back yard and filled the garden beds. Katy would wait until the grass was far too high before cutting it. Then she would scalp the lawn with her unsharpened mower blades. Nothing on her side would ever get watered because of course she would have to pay her share for the water. I had to pay for a tree firm to come bring a watering truck to deep root water the large front tree or I risked losing it.

As a preventive measure every second year the sewer line would be augered at my expense. But as soon as one of the lower tenants advised me that their sink drains were running too slowly I would have the sewer lines checked and augered again. It was necessary to prevent possible back up damage.

UNENDING NOISE & TENANT PROBLEMS

The way the lower suites had been constructed placed their bedrooms under the living rooms of the upper suites. The living rooms of the lower suites were under the upper suite bedrooms. Big mistake. The bedroom ceilings had been dry walled without any extra sound insulation between the joists.

Katy lived on one upper side. She worked late night hours at a bar. She had been there for about six years. When I inspected her suite with the vendor I saw that she had a great many possessions and an old cat. Her rent was always paid on time, I was told. I couldn't increase her security deposit to cover one month's current rent or take one for her pet. The law did not allow changes to the initial security deposit.

The quiet older man who had just moved in moved out without staying more than a month. He said there was too much noise from upstairs. I re-rented his suite to a young couple. They stayed only until the end of their six month lease. Through the rapid turnover of tenants that I rented the lower suite to, it became apparent that there was a noise problem. I hired a handyman who took down the T bar ceiling in the lower suite living room and kitchen, stuffed the shallow cavity with added insulation and put it back up. I didn't do anything to the dry walled ceilings in the bedrooms.

INCOMPATIBLE TENANTS

I then tried to be extra careful about who I rented to, hoping they would be compatible with Katy. I interviewed at length one of two young musicians that became tenants under Katy. I was assured that they would use their earplugs when they played at night. The second musician tenant didn't. He would play his electric guitar at 3 am if he wanted. Katy would pound on the floor and then began shutting off the heat to the basement. Then the serious battles began and I found myself embroiled in a war. I spoke with both tenants and even wrote them letters to respect each other. All to no avail. The young men even called the Police to have Katy stop pounding on the floor, disturbing them in the middle of the night. I finally had to ask the young men to leave.

Next a lovely black couple recently emigrating from an island near Africa moved in with their 13 year old son. When they applied I noted how soft spoken and quiet they were. The husband and wife were both security guards. He spoke French and was applying for a librarian position. I had contacted their current landlord since they were leaving their previous location without a full month's notice. She indicated that it was fine with her.

I let the family move in part way through the month. When I gave the required 24 hour notice to bring in new furnace filters, I was shocked. The family had virtually no possessions. There was a TV and one plastic chair in the living room. Several mattresses were lying on the bedroom floors, with clothing in heaps nearby. A worn out old arborite kitchen table with three totally disreputable torn old vinyl chairs with stuffing sticking out were the only furnishings in the kitchen. I realized that that was why the previous landlord had granted them an early leave. She would not have been able to show her space to new tenants with that scruffy furniture there.

I began to think Katy was prejudiced because the African tenants were colored. Almost right away the problems began. Katy began harassing the new tenants. She began rattling boxes and thumping on the adjoining basement entry door, which terrified the quiet wife downstairs. Katy would run all the hot water into her tub until the water tank was cold just before the couple came home from work. Then I would receive complaints that there was no hot water. Katy controlled the thermostat for the whole side. She would turn the heat down so low upstairs that the family below was freezing cold. I bought them an oil filled heater to help. Again in frustration I tried to reason with Katy and sent her letters which she ignored or disputed.

On sunny days Katy took to lying out on the rear patio in a skimpy bikini. The African couple found it offensive since she was lying right outside their living room windows. By now I was trying to build a case to evict her. But Katy in turn was insisting that the suite downstairs was illegal and she would call the authorities to get the family evicted. She really wanted the whole place to herself but at no increase in rent.

SKIPPING OUT

Within several months the rent check from the African couple didn't clear the bank. I notified the couple of the NSF and received an apology and another check in replacement. When asked, the man told me everything was okay. When that second check also didn't clear I went to the duplex and realized that they had skipped. I called their employer who told me that they had given their notice and moved back to Africa.

When I entered the now vacant suite I discovered all their junk furniture was still there, along with most of the heaps of clothing. Not only had Katy scared them away but a letter on the fridge top told the story. The letter was from the government cancelling the man's driving license. I felt sorry for them. Without a license neither one would have been able to get to work. Their only decent possession was their TV. It was a nice one in a wooden cabinet that I was able to trade for the carpet cleaning. To have their usable clothing taken to Good Will and remaining clothing and possessions hauled to the dump became my expense.

CONTINUING HARASSMENT

Next I found a nice older single lady who I'll call Rose, to live downstairs under Katy. Rose was timid and sweet. When the complaints began again about the heat I had a second thermostat installed downstairs. Now Rose below could also control the heat. Katy complained that she was too hot upstairs now.

Then the noise problems began again. When Katy came home late at night she would purposely thump around her living room above Rose's bedroom. This would go on sometimes until 4 am when Katy would go to bed. This prevented Rose downstairs from sleeping. Rose had to get up at 5:30 am to go to work. Katy would sleep during the daytime. Pretty soon there was a fight going on. Katy upstairs would make even more deliberate noise. Rose, beginning to be desperate for sleep, had her son go to talk to Katy, but to no avail.

I began to receive long letters from Rose. Each time I would send a letter to Katy to stop her excessive noise. She would respond with a complaint that Rose did not pay her share of the utilities in a timely manner. To end that situation I took over paying the utilities for Rose and collected back from her instead.

THE FAILED EVICTION

Rose was becoming increasingly depressed and afraid of Katy. It began disturbing me too. I finally felt I had enough written complaints from Rose to get Katy evicted even though her lease had another six months to run. I gave Katy a fifteen day eviction notice. However Katy didn't move out when the fifteen days were up. So then I hired a law firm and began another eviction process through the courts.

Rose had put up with months of Katy's bad behavior but was now almost at a breakdown point from lack of sleep. Rose's daughter gave Rose courage to take action. Rose couldn't take the stress any more. Mild Rose began thumping with a broom handle on the ceiling under Katy's bedroom at 5:30 in the morning. That action seemed to quiet Katy for a while.

The lawyer, however, said Rose's actions had blown my legal case to have Katy removed. I had to drop it and pay the $600.00 legal bill. At that point I had had enough aggravation and put the building up for sale. I figured that I was just not cut out to be a landlord of this type of aggravating dwelling.

"Litigation is expensive, time consuming and to be avoided."

Keith and Sandi Cunningham

NON TROUBLE FREE OTHER SIDE

During this time I had also experienced problems on the other side of the duplex.

Common law tenants who had been living in the upper suite had been there several years. Then one day they had a knock out drag down fight and damaged the place. The couple separated and moved out in the middle of the night, still owing me rent. Among the mess and damage were holes kicked into several doors. They left a badly stained and damaged carpet that I was forced to replace. I managed to track down the woman through her employment at a restaurant. I hired a collection agency who tried to recover my lost rent and $1,600.00 of repair expenses. Soon however the agency advised that the woman had filed for bankruptcy and I couldn't collect a nickel.

When they moved out a young common law couple with a new baby, who had been living downstairs under Katy on the other side were allowed to move in. Soon they separated leaving just the young man, I will call Tom, in the suite. Tom moved in another man to share the cost with him and continued to rent. He would pay his rent late and penalties built up. Tom said he loved to paint and he would paint the rear deck in exchange for the penalty. I agreed, bought the paint for the balcony and gave it to him. I had to keep reminding him to get the job done when summer came and the painting dragged on untouched. Finally he did paint the deck doing a reasonable job of it.

Then Tom gave his notice, saying that he had purchased a small house nearby. When I made my inspection there was an alarming amount of smoky paint damage. It had been caused by heavy smoking of suspected drugs and improper use of the fireplace. I agreed to let Tom repaint when he pleaded to recover his damage deposit. I bought 5 gallons of paint for $110.00 and gave it to the tenant to do the work. Instead he stole the paint to use in his new house! Obviously I withheld his deposit but it didn't cover the damage as well as his delinquent rent.

I then had to hire a painter and eat the cost when I couldn't recover it. It was very time consuming and difficult to recover losses through small claims court at that time. Now a new arbitration process was recently started in our area that can make recovery assessments or settle tenant landlord problems easier and faster at minimal cost.

A HURRIED RENTAL IS A MISTAKE

"Beware of tenants with good stories...Be skeptical."

Keith and Sandi Cunningham

I made the mistake of renting out the upper space in a hurry. It had been vacant most of the month and I was facing a second vacant month. I wanted to recoup my loss quickly.

A family of three with a cat were moving from another city. They needed a space in a hurry so the father could start a new job right away. They filled out an application that indicated reasonable income. I called the local employer where the man was going to be working. Since he had previously worked there as a seasonal employee I received a good report. I also received a good report when I checked the family's personal reference. While the references gave good reports I couldn't reach the previous landlord at all. When the credit report came back showing nothing I didn't realize that it was a red flag and agreed to let them move in.

The couple said they did not have more than $200.00 to start but would pay me the balance the next Friday. I foolishly agreed but did collect the remainder the following week. I had added a deposit for the cat to the security deposit to be paid as well.

Built into my leases was a daily penalty clause for paying rent late. Almost right away I had to enforce this clause and collected penalties for several month's late rent. The tenant's payments were always tardy. When the late rent and NSF's started I would give eviction notices to them on the third day or as soon as I received word from the bank about the NSF. I even went to the wife's employment to take her to her bank to get me the rent. She took out money but kept several hundred dollars for herself, giving me only half the rent.

On one of my visits to collect rent the wife told me she had just bought a new bedroom set. I was seething! She could buy new furniture but not pay her rent to me. When I gave notice for late rent the next month they skipped out, owing me over a month's rent and penalties. I couldn't begin an action to recover because I didn't know where they had gone. Without an address I couldn't have the summons papers served. I also discovered that they had used an assumed name on their utility bills.

UNPAID UTILTIES

In another incident on that side of the duplex the tenant upstairs stopped paying the utilities. I found out only when the power was shut off to that side and the lower tenant complained to me. The lower tenant said they had always paid their share to the upper tenant every month. When I contacted the utility company they did not want to restart the services unless I paid the account which was several months overdue and over $400.00 in arrears.

DERELICT PICK UP TRUCK

That same tenant moved out leaving a derelict pickup truck blocking the rear driveway to one of the garages. Before abandoning the vehicle he had stripped off most useable parts. I had quite a problem to get the City bylaw officer to take any action because the truck was on my parking pad, my private property. The bylaw officer said that the property required signage allowing vehicles to be towed from private property. It took several bylaw notifications posted on the vehicle and several of my trips to meet the bylaw officers before they finally had it hauled away. That tenant also took away the remote opener for the garage door. I hadn't remembered to put it on the condition report or get a deposit for it. I was resigned to just being out of pocket.

CALLING IT QUITS: THE SALE

I was oh so ready to sell. The virtually identical duplex with suites next door to mine was listed for sale at the time. I called the listing Realtor who agreed with me that the likely selling price would be quite a bit lower than the present listed price. I then set my price based on that number. I was selling the building myself. Having separate titles enabled me to sell each side more easily. Separate titles gave each side a higher value in the marketplace.

While the duplex next door was similar to mine, it did not have any single garages; mine had two. I forgot that difference when I priced my duplex. I realized too late that I had short changed myself by at least $25,000.00 on my sale price. However I was relieved to sell quickly. In retrospect, had I used a Realtor I would have received a much higher price.

When I was showing Katy's suite to prospective purchasers I was shocked to see that she now had one bedroom filled almost to the ceiling with her possessions. Her garage was also totally stuffed with things. She had become a pack rat. An experienced purchaser would have shied away from the sale upon seeing that. They would have anticipated the cost of disposal of all the things that would be left behind. But my price was attractive and the purchasers accepted it.

I advised the purchasing couple about the problems with Katy. I told them not to renew her lease. They were fortunate. She bought her own place and moved out when her lease ended several months later. To my surprise I was told she even left her suite empty and clean.

RENTING TIPS

BEST TIMES TO ADVERTISE

Advertise from the 1st day to the 9th day. Then don't advertise between the 10th to the 19th. Then begin your ad again from the 19th day to the end of the month. Be careful with mid month rentals. Tenants seeking spaces at the middle of the month may have been evicted on a 15 day notice. Good potential tenants will have given their one months notice. At the first of the month they will begin looking seriously. If they haven't found something by the last week they may be readier to rent.

Get window signs made up to display in a street view window. The sign may be all you require to find tenants in a good rental area.

TELEPHONE TIPS

For prospective tenant interviews

Spend time to write out your own question list and use it with each caller responding to your sign or ad. You want to eliminate arranging showings of your property to unqualified renters.

Tim Johnson had a very good telephone system for evaluating and showing tenants. He pointed out that whoever is asking the questions is in control of the conversation. You want to keep control to save your time. The caller will try to get you to answer his questions unless you ask first and keep asking your questions.

At any point that the renter's answers don't fit your criteria thank them and end the conversation. Whenever a reply doesn't sound right you can either end the conversation or get more clarification. After getting a questionable answer sometimes you can encourage more information by just saying "Uh Huh' and keeping silent.

Listen to how they sound as they answer your questions. Are they open or guarded with their replies? Are they being flippant or sincere? Remember that you are using the telephone to begin your evaluation of a tenant.

1. Start by asking the renter how soon they need a place to rent. This question will help you to determine whether to continue the conversation or not. If they are looking for future dates you could ask if they would like to be contacted if you have an opening at that time. Then take down their name and address for your waiting list.

2. Get information right away about how many people will be occupying the space and whether they have any pets. If you have a restriction on either numbers of occupants or pets tell them. If you require a pet deposit mention it.

3. If you only rent on long term leases it will assist you to find out how long they plan to rent for. Find out how long they have been living at their current address and whether they have given notice to their current landlord. If they haven't given proper notice to their landlord chances are that they won't give you proper notice either.

4. Tell the renter how much your security deposit is and that it must be paid in cash with the application. Listen to their response. If their reply sounds doubtful or that they do not have the money, this would be a good time to end your conversation. You could suggest that they try other ways to get the money from relatives or credit cards if you wish.

   Renters that have any problem with providing the security deposit will likely cause you grief down the road when they fail to pay or are late with the rent. It is never a good idea to begin playing banker.

   When I let my heart rule my head by not getting cash up front it certainly cost me. I had a constant collection battle from then on until the tenants skipped owing me money.

5. Ask about the renter's employment. This will give you an idea of their ability to pay the rent. If they are not employed try to get enough detail to help you make a decision.

6. If it is early in the month you may wish to ask whether they are serious or are still getting a feeling for what is in the rental market. If they are still just fact finding you may wish to thank them and hang up. If the renter's answers have made them a serious prospect only then do you want to discuss showing them the space.

7. It is useful to ask where they obtained your telephone number so that you can determine which type of advertising is the most effective to place in the future.

8. Next arrange the showing date and time. One of the biggest problems with arranging showings of the property is "no shows" especially if you have driven across town to open the property. The incidents of "no shows" can be greatly reduced

if you set a date for a specific future time but indicate that you will only come at the appointed time if they will call you a half hour ahead on that day to reconfirm their attendance.

9. At this point in your telephone conversation you want to make certain that they write down your name and telephone number as well as the property address on something that they can find again. Remember that renters will call a number of ads at the same time and may forget which ad is yours.

SHOWING TIPS

1. If you find it convenient to do so you can arrange multiple showings for the same appointment time. Remember that some prospects may not appear or call you ahead as prearranged. In addition competition for your desirable space may lead to an immediate decision to rent instead of a wait to see what's on the market attitude.

2. If all your prospective renters show up at the same time give each an application form if they say they are interested. Select one prospective renter to tour with you while the others wait outside or in another room filling out their applications.

3. When you collect the filled out applications review them with each prospect to make certain they have completely filled out their pertinent and reference information. Remember that you will need a correctly spelled name and birth date and current address to obtain a credit rating.

4. If they are interested take a cash deposit. If they don't have cash on them a good prospect will immediately arrange to get to their bank and return with the money. If several are interested you may take a deposit from each potential renter advising them that it will be refunded immediately if they are not selected after you check their references.

156

5. Do not ever spend the time to get your application filled out without obtaining a deposit at the same time. Prospective tenants without a deposit are not serious.

BUYING TIPS & EXPENSIVE LESSONS:

1. Once again do thorough due diligence before you purchase. Check everything you possibly can. Review easements on title, allowable zoning, real property report indications of any easements, pending government or city work that could affect your property, etc. does the survey show the fence line to be on the property boundary or do you wholly own it? Check with the bylaw department whether there are any unsatisfied issues or pending rulings that have been issued against the property.

2. You may also want to spend a bit of time in the neighborhood during both daytime and evening to see what types of people live in the area.

3. Hire an inspector to inspect the property thoroughly. Get an estimate of any suggested deficiencies before signing off your sales conditions.

4. If the property has a wood-burning fireplace have it inspected, including the chimney. Creosote build up in a chimney can cause serious chimney fires. Tenants may burn garbage or scrap wood in the fireplace which can create a very hot fire and add to the potential danger.

5. Don't ever provide a personal guarantee if you can help it. In adverse conditions a personal guarantee could cost your own home or other investments.

6. Be fully aware that if you buy an illegal suited property that the city could close your illegal suites in the event of a complaint. Secondary suites are now being encouraged in many older areas but there will be building requirements to be met. Some can be expensive to implement after a residence has been constructed.

7. Read the mortgage documents or contact the lender to find out about any early payout penalty costs. By blending an old mortgage with a newer one you can often reduce the interest rate of the mortgage.

8. Is there sufficient off street parking for each unit? If the property has parking spaces outside that are on a laneway, consider putting up bylaw approved parking signs to enable vehicles to be towed from common property.

9. Do a risk management inspection. Look carefully to spot potential problems on the site such as a heaved sidewalk that could be a trip hazard or a liability issue and plan to have it repaired. Check around the foundation of the building for any areas that would allow water to seep in due to negative sloping. Most insurance clauses will not pay for seepage water losses.

10. Up and down suites each require their own heating or individually controlled furnace system. If the building you are contemplating purchasing has only one furnace for two suites it may not be possible to add an additional exhaust flue for a second furnace. Have a furnace company check it out.

11. In the case of upper and lower suites ensure that the window openings are of sufficient size to meet bylaw requirements for light, air and fire escape purposes.

12. In your financial plan set up a vacancy allowance. This should be based on the current vacancy rate in your area. Banks often apply a 5% rate when they are calculating the rent return for a new mortgage.

13. It is not a good idea to allow tenants to paint their suite. They may paint unsuitable colors and ruin the woodwork or carpets with paint spills.

14. Sell using a Realtor to help you set your price and do the negotiations. A middle man is worth the price.

15. Try as you may to avoid it, you may find you have a Katy type of tenant. Know the law and what steps you may take.

16. Sewer lines in older buildings can be a problem. Because underground sewer lines running into older homes were often made of clay tile with joints, tree roots can get into the pipes through the joints. If maintenance of a sewer line problem becomes extreme a new line may be able to be inserted into the sewer line from the street without tearing up the complete lawn area.

RENTAL TIPS

1. Obtain the approved forms for preparing a detailed condition report from the municipality's rental department. Fill it in with the tenant and use the same form again when they move out. Make certain you obtain the tenant's signatures on the move in form so that there are no arguments about unlisted damages when the tenant moves out.

2. Hold yourself back from renting until you find the right tenant. Plan on being vacant an extra month if necessary until you find and check out potential tenants.

3. Good questions to put on your application to rent are:

- Have you ever declared bankruptcy?
- Are you willing to keep your stereo volume down out of consideration for other residents?
- What kind and how many vehicles do you have?
- What are their vehicle license numbers?

4. Determine whether your building is to be non smoking or not and add lease wording. Post small appropriate signs at the suite entrances.

5. A credit report with nothing on it is a red flag. A credit report with any judgments on it is also. Do more checking about the circumstances or do not rent to that person. In order to obtain a credit report you will require the potential tenant's name, date of birth, and ideally social insurance number.

6. When there are shared utilities it will be best if you pay one of the portions and get reimbursed by the appropriate tenant. This eliminates tenant disagreements from festering into bigger problems. Do use a utility agreement form that specifies the percentage share to be paid by each party.

7. Make certain that you obtain landlord insurance and that your tenants initial the lease statement to acknowledge their responsibility to obtain tenant insurance or insist that they provide you with a copy or an insurance certificate.

8. Minimize maintenance expense by offering incentives to the tenants to look after the maintenance. Write your lease for a higher amount and build in a reduction for being a good tenant and performing certain specific work. Write your lease clause wording to reference the specific terms of being a good tenant. Things like paying rent on time, cleaning up waste after pets, keeping the grounds watered and weeded, etc. If the work is not completed put in that the higher rent rate automatically becomes due. Since it is incorporated in your lease you should be able to enforce it.

All my mistakes in the stock market are highlighted for your review and edification in Chapter 11.

Rental forms follow:

RENTAL APPLICATION (address)_____Date:___

Name:_____Date of birth:_____
Please print: Last   First

Home phone _____**Work phone**_____
Best time to call_____

Present Address

_____

Rented or owned _____ How long resided there_____
Rent $_____
Owner/Manager_____ Owner/ Manager phone: _____
Reason for moving

_____

Previous address

_____

Rented or owned _____ How long resided there_____
Rent $_____
Owner/Manager_____ Owner/ Manager phone: _____
Reason for moving

_____

Name, relationship and age of every person to live with you

_____

_____

_____

Any pets? _____Describe_____

Do you own a high-fidelity stereo?_____ Are you willing to modulate the sound in consideration of others?_____

Present occupation: _____

Employer & Phone Number: _____
Supervisor & Phone number: _____

How long with this employer:_____

Current gross income per month $_____

Amount of alimony or child support you pay $____or receive $_____

Make of Vehicle _____Model & color_____
Year_____License No. _____Insured with_____

Savings account
Bank_____

Branch _____

Chequing account
Bank_____

Branch _____

Do you have a Major Credit card _____

Have you ever filed bankruptcy? _____

Have you ever been evicted?_____

Personal Reference Name
_____

Address_____
Phone_____

Emergency Contact

Address:_____Phone:_____

The above information is strictly confidential; however, a CREDIT

CHECK will be made on all applicants. I hereby warrant that above

information is correct and give my permission for the landlord to do

a credit check.

Dated this_____ day of_____,20 ____

Witness _____

Signature of Applicant:_____

ACCEPTANCE OF UTILITIES & SMOKE DETECTOR AGREEMENT

I/We_____, understand that I/We are responsible for transferring all utilities for the rental premises at

_____

over to my/our name(s) as of our move-in date WITH THE EXCEPTION OF THOSE CIRCLED BELOW:

WATER/SEWER   WASTE   HEAT   ELECTRICITY   CABLE   PHONE

Transferring the utilities is a condition of tenancy and I/we understand that failure to do so within a reasonabler time will be considered a breach of my/our tenancy agrement.

I/We also acknowledge that _____smoke detector(s) installed in the premises are in good working order. I/we agree to maintain the smoke detector(s) in good working order during our tenancy.

Dated at _____this _____day of_____200__

_____   _____
Tenant   Witness

_____   _____
Tenant   Witness

CHAPTER 11

HOW *NOT* TO INVEST IN THE STOCK MARKET

Commissions take their bite; Investment newsletters can mislead; Market moves & trends; Forecasting methods; Master your emotions; Learn what you need to know; Learn when to sell

"Investment must be rational; if you don't understand it

don't do it"

Warren Buffett

Are you going to select stocks because their earning values are always rising and compounding or will you buy "out of favor' stocks in hopes that the shares will become popular again and share prices will increase in value? Or are you looking for stocks that provide regular income through dividend payments? Again, your investment plan is of importance.

HOW *NOT* TO INVEST IN THE STOCK MARKET

"With enough inside information and a million dollars, you can go broke in a year."

Warren Buffet

Investing in stocks is not something to blithely go into. No matter what hot tip, broker advice, or newsletter comment received, to enter the market not knowing what to do is very costly. While I had made money buying and holding real estate, I knew nothing of the stock market. I had an intuitive sense about properties that I would buy, but no sense at all for the stock market. It took me several years to learn the basics of investing in stocks. I never did learn about investing in options, which many use to make good money. Of course I have lost money quite a few times. Take my advice and save yourself from the same pitfalls.

According to James Dines, a respected investment newsletter writer, gamblers in the stock market have an inner desire to lose money. That would explain why we buy high and sell low instead of the other way around. The successful players buy shortly after an upturn starting from a low and sell shortly after a downturn starting from a high.

My first mistake was to take the advice of a friend. A company he worked for in a senior position was about to declare news that he said would certainly increase the company's share value. I bought some shares in his company through a broker. The shares did not go up and I lost money.

EXPENSIVE LESSON

Do not accept hot tips. By the time you hear about it the timing is already too late, especially if it has been reported in newspapers.

When I reentered the market my biggest mistake was to not learn about how the stock market functions. I bought in blindly, some on the advice of my broker, knowing nothing about how to invest wisely in the market. I had no plan for when to sell. I did not know what types of investment vehicles are available, or what I wanted to get from investing in the market.

VARIOUS INVESTMENT VEHICLES

Learn about the various types of stocks, E.T.F's (exchange traded funds), limited trusts, hedge funds, index funds, mutual funds, bonds, and derivatives. What are they composed of? How do you earn money through holding a particular type of investment? It is good to understand whether the vehicle you are considering is in a higher risk category or not.

STOCK EXCHANGE NAMES

It took me quite a while to get the stock market names fixed to their call letters let alone to what they trade in. There are a great many more exchanges with sub groups. It is useful to know what types of stocks are traded in each market. For instance TSX Venture sells small cap types of shares. Many are start-up small capitalization companies with low cost but high risk share prices. Names and call letters of a few markets are:

- American Stock Exchange (AMEX)
- New York Stock Exchange (NYSE) or often referred to as "Wall Street"
- National Association of Security Dealers Automated Quotation System (NASDAQ)
- Toronto Stock Exchange (TSX)
- Toronto Stock Venture Exchange (TSXV)
- Dow Jones Industrial Average (DJI or the Dow)
- Dow Jones Transportation Average (DJT)
- Dow Jones Utility Average (DJU)
- Dow Jones Corporate Bond Average (DJCB)
- Standard & Poors 500 Composite (SPX)
- IW Internet Index (IIX)
- FTSE International is the London Stock Exchange
- (ASX) is the Australian Securities Exchange
- (HANG SENG) is a Hong Kong Exchange
- (NIKKEI) is a Japanese Exchange
- (XETRA DAX) is a German Exchange
- SHENZEN) is a Chinese exchange

EXPENSIVE LESSONS:

Before investing learn about how the market functions and what to do. Here is a check list.

1. What are your investing goals? Write them down.

2. How much risk are you comfortable with? What is your investing personality?

3. Are you a buy and hold investor? Are you going to be a value investor looking for undervalued stocks?

4. A contrarian investor? One who buys or sells opposite the broker's advice?

5. Are you are just trying for quick short term capital gain? Do you plan to be a day trader?

6. Are you are seeking income or regular dividend payments?

7. Or do you plan to be a growth investor looking for long term growth stocks to hold.

8. Which vehicle is the best fit for your comfort zone and your goals?

9. It is critical to design a selling plan before you ever buy stocks.

10. Learn how to evaluate a prospective stock company. Do your due diligence on the company you select to invest in. Check with Sedar.com to obtain financial information. Call   to speak with the company's investor relations person.

   • What kind of opportunity is it?
   • Is it a start up company with an initial offering?
   • What does the company do? Is its product unique?
   • Who are its competitors?
   • Are its sales figures growing or declining?

- Is it making a profit that is growing?
- Is it making money or losing money?
- What percentage of stock is owned by management?

11. Each stock you hold will require more or less of your time to track in order to keep current. How much time a day or a week do you intend to devote to investing?

12. How will you keep in touch with the market? Will you invest in a computer tracking service? Will you hire a broker to look after your account?

13. Learn how to read stock performance charts. Sign up for a free stock news service like www.globaladvisor.com

14. Learn about the various methods of valuing stocks such as P/E ratios (price divided by earnings)

15. Learn about methods of determining when to buy and sell using technical forecasting trends and/or fundamentals or combination formulas.

16. Set an upside gain goal (perhaps 10% or 20% higher than purchase price). When your stock reaches that goal sell it or reset your next goal if the gaining trend is continuing.

17. How much are you willing to lose? Learn about stops and trailing stops. Determine appropriate percentage stops (perhaps 10% lower) to place below your purchase price for your protection.

18. Realize the risk. If a sudden drop in share price occurs the gap down may bypass your stop without triggering a sale.

19. Do not become emotionally connected to your stock. You will resist selling it when you should sell.

COMMISSIONS TAKE THEIR BITE

Having at last accumulated a little money to invest following the sale of some properties, I wanted to shelter it from capital gains tax. I put a large chunk of money aside and transferred it along with a private investment into a new RSP (tax deferred) account with a large brokerage firm. Then on the broker's advice I bought some stocks. All but one of these stocks failed me. For each stock purchase or sale I sadly learned that my minimum commission was $95.00 a trade or more. The broker gained but I lost.

EXPENSIVE LESSONS:

1. How much commission will it cost you to buy and sell your shares?

2. Consider doing your own trading on the internet. Costs are considerably less at from $3.00 to $29.00 per trade.

3. Brokers push stocks in order to make their commission. The stocks they promote are not always right for you. Some people have become wealthy being contrarian by doing the opposite to the broker's advice.

"Clearly, a hugely important element of successful trading is knowing what information is of value, which sources can be trusted, and what should be taken with a grain of salt."

John Forman author of "Essential Trading"

INVESTMENT NEWS LETTERS CAN MISLEAD

I signed up for a stock market newsletter whose advice had enabled a friend to treble his money. The newsletter listed suggested stocks to buy in five different categories of risk.

1. The first grade suggested moderate capital gains, moderate risk, moderate income, and good long term fundamentals.

2. The second list indicated long term growth, large capital gains, moderate risk, low income and strong long term fundamentals.

3. The third category was precious metals.

4. The fourth grade was for nearer term stocks with high risk and high potential gains.

5. The last grade included low priced stocks with very high risk and very high potential capital gains.

The newsletter's focus was primarily on commodities and uranium mining. In the least risk category were stocks I felt were too expensive to buy. They were all over $30.00 a share or more. I began buying uranium mining stocks suggested in the lower two priced lists. I purchased from pennies up to $8.00 a share. These stocks were much higher risk but offered high potential rewards. Knowing nothing about the companies whose stock I was purchasing, I just picked names from an investment club list that I had seen.

EXPENSIVE LESSONS:

1. One problem of using a popular newsletter as your guide to selecting stock shares is that many other people are also following the same newsletter's advice. By the time you realize to act on the recommendation the purchases by others have already inflated the price you pay.

2. Owning stock of exploration mining companies is very risky since they have no earnings, only expenditures. Even if they find a very good potential mine site it takes many dollars and many years

before the company will have any earnings. Meanwhile every time they have a stock offering or give options on shares to their employees your share value becomes diluted.

CONFUSING CONTRARY MARKET MOVES

I learned the hard way as I watched the ups and downs of my stock portfolio. On good news the market goes down and on bad news the market goes up.

EXPENSIVE LESSON:

1. The moves of the market are irrational. They are often opposite to what you would expect. Fear and greed run the markets. Buy on the rumor; sell on the fact is not easy to do.

2. In today's markets you are also betting against the huge transactions made by various funds that can alter the market quickly. With the buyers and sellers all using computers the market values can change very quickly.

OH OH! MARKETS ARE SEASONAL

One of my early mistakes was in not knowing that there is a seasonal buying market in stock markets. My initial purchases were made in May when traditionally the big corporate investors sell off shares before going for summer holidays which generally causes prices to go down.

EXPENSIVE LESSON:

The markets make seasonal moves especially noticeable in May. In December there can also be a sell off period while investors take their tax losses before the year end.

MARKET TRENDS CAN BE MYSTERIOUS

I saw my stocks moving down and sold some quickly with no plan or knowledge about trends. After falling a few points these stocks rose again but having already sold I lost out. Then as they rose again I would buy in again. I didn't realize that the stocks were in a consolidation trend and that they were moving up and down in a pattern. I had not mastered the intricacies of market forecasting.

EXPENSIVE LESSON:

Learn to understand the different forecasting trends and patterns.

TOO MANY FORECASTING METHODS

Many systems with variations have been developed to assist in determining the best time to buy or sell stocks. It is imperative to learn how to read and understand stock charts. The easiest way is to subscribe to a good forecasting software program such as Investools. They will provide a tutorial that can be a valuable teaching aid. A software program that builds in information from a number of forecast methods will provide a simplified forecasting tool that can save you much time.

TECHNICAL ANALYSIS CHART TERMS CAN BE CONFUSING

"Master a formula and then learn a new one."

Robert T. Kiyosaki

Technical analysis incorporates charts or graphs to analyze investments in an attempt to predict the future. Technical analysis

174

studies price and volume of sales. It is really tracking what people think the stocks are worth by buying or selling them. These include an overlay of a selection of forecasting methods. I had no idea what they meant when I began buying stocks. Here is a description of a few of these:

- **Moving averages**: These lines on a chart show the 'average' value over set periods of time. They are trend following indicators to identify trend changes over a period of time. For instance one line may chart 50 week averages and the second line 200 week averages. Where they cross each other can be a buying or selling signal. It is considered bearish if it crosses on the down side and bullish if it crosses on the upside.
- **Bollinger bands**: An overlay that show the upper and lower limits of 'normal' price movements that are based on volatility.
- **MACD**: means the 'moving average convergence divergence' of two lines that show the momentum and direction of a stocks' movement. MACD is a trend following indicator used to identify trend changes. It indicates the difference between fast and slow exponential moving averages of closing prices. It is based on a set of numbers each of which is the average of a corresponding subset of a larger set of data points. It is used in a time series to smooth out short term fluctuations and to highlight longer term trends or cycles. The signal line is most often set to record changes for a nine day period but can be set for other periods. When the MACD line crosses over the trigger or signal line it can indicate a time to buy or sell based on the direction of its movement.
- **Candlesticks:** These are daily indicators of the highest and lowest selling price of a specific stock on a given day. Using the candlestick formation for showing the trend line is very useful. Technical analysts have learned to follow patterns based on candlestick shapes that can be used as indicators of trend changes. Lines drawn between the tops or bottoms of the candlestick groups can indicate a trend.

- **Volume:** of sales is shown in a vertical bar graph form and indicates the amount of activity (number of shares traded) on a specific day. A great deal of activity will indicate a direction of price change movement.
- **Insider trading:** If the principals in a company are selling their shares there may be reason to be concerned. Certain types of explanations are required to be filed with SEDAR.
- **Industry class:** is not always shown on a stock chart but is worth checking. If a stock is in an industry group that is performing well an individual stock in that group may do better than if the industry group is performing poorly. Charting software will provide this information.
- **Resistance and support levels:** These are based on emotional expectations of buyers and sellers. They are created by drawing lines to connect the tops and bottoms of the highest and lowest sales points on a chart. The highest sales line is the resistance line. The line drawn between the lowest sales prices is the support line.

The resistance line indicates the highest price a buyer will pay. In other words they resist paying any more than the previously paid top price.

The support line is the lowest price that sellers will sell their stock for; therefore they support the lowest price.

When the resistance line is broken through with an even higher price then the old resistance line becomes the new support line. It creates an expectation of even higher prices to come. In the same manner when the support line is breached investors anticipate lower prices will follow.

Master the meanings of key indicators on a chart. Learn how they point to market trends. Use them to guide your buying and selling.

WATCH THE CHANGE IN TRENDS

Watch the stock charts. Only buy after stocks have begun a real uptrend. If the uptrend continues, reset your upper selling limit goal and your protective selling stop higher. After the trend reverses and begins moving downward, sell. To avoid false moves   don't try to guess when the trend has changed direction but catch it shortly after it has changed, then buy or sell. Internet stock market tools such as Big Charts, Investools and others can make your decisions easier.

SELLING TOO SOON CAN BE COSTLY

I was reacting to watching the market every day but not really knowing what I was seeing. I was selling too soon or buying at the wrong time.

EXPENSIVE LESSON:

You may trade stocks too often if you watch your stocks every day. Purchase your stocks with care then watching them daily is only necessary if you plan to become a day trader.

MASTER YOUR EMOTIONS OR YOU WILL LOSE

"A stock doesn't know that you own it."

Warren Buffett

Because I believed strongly in their potential, I also purchased stocks in a biotech company. I loved using their products and became emotionally attached. Initially my biotech stocks went up more than a dollar above the $3.00 I had paid. I didn't realize that I should sell and take my profit. Soon the company's expansion program failed and the stocks plummeted to $0.56 a share. Because I was emotionally attached I still didn't sell. Now they are at only $.36 a share. Sigh!

EXPENSIVE LESSON:

Do not allow yourself to become attached emotionally to a stock. You will not let go and may hold it too long. Set your gain selling point and stop losses in advance and follow through on them.

LEARN HOW FEAR & GREED CAN FORECAST
WHEN TO SELL

I did not realize what a large role emotions play in what happens in the markets. Fear and greed appear to be the main motivation of buyers. There is a type of pattern to the fear and greed cycle that a wise investor can learn.

EXPENSIVE LESSON:

When everyone is buying it is time to get out because greed will push stock prices beyond their real value. Indicated by their stock price to earnings ratio (P/E ratio). When everyone is fearful and stocks are below value it is time to buy in, of course after having done your due diligence. James Dine's book ***"How to Make Money using MASS PSYCHOLOGY"*** can aid your understanding of how fear and greed affect the market and what to watch for.

WISE INVESTORS WATCH INDUSTRY GROUPS

When I purchased stock in the biotech company, it was not a good time to buy a biotech stock. By consulting Investools before making my purchase I could have learned that the biotech industry group was not doing well. I hadn't known the importance of this and other trading information that was available.

Investools could have shown me averages, stock sales volumes, insider and commercial trading and a summary of other market indicators including price to earnings ratios, etc, that would have shown me in minutes whether it was a good time to buy the stock. It also would have given indicators telling me when to sell.

EXPENSIVE LESSON:

Review various investment guidance tools available such as Investools and consult them before buying or selling.

-

SO MUCH INFORMATION TO PLOW THROUGH

I began to receive financial statements from mining companies in the mail but found the information confusing to understand. Because so much was reported on I did not know what items were important.

EXPENSIVE LESSON:

Learn what financial information is important to know. The best financial guide I have found is the excellent book called *"Warren Buffet and the Interpretation of Financial Statements"* by Mary Buffett and David Clark. They teach the fundamentals of how to determine whether a company is one that you should consider investing in.

AND THEN THERE ARE OPTIONS

Buying options can enable a trader to make money using more leverage. First they must have a margin account with a broker. I found the terminology confusing and never tried to buy options. Some people do well with options but my friend Ann tried and tried without success.

The word "call" is short for "call option", a right to buy stock. This is a contract with a specific time limit that gives the right to a buyer to purchase a set number of shares from a seller at a date in the future. The buyer has the right to buy at the option price but is not obligated to exercise the option. Buyers of a call option believe that the stock's price will rise within a set time period. A "call" means a right to buy if you are a buyer; or an obligation to sell if you are a seller.

The word "put" is short for "put option" a right to sell a stock. This is a contract giving the option buyer the right to sell a stock at a predetermined price on or before a specific date. If the option is exercised the "put" requires the seller to sell an agreed number of shares to a buyer at a set predetermined price. A "put" gives the right to sell to a buyer and is an obligation to sell to the buyer if one is the seller.

When a person buys a "call" they believe the shares will go up in value to the exercise price called the "strike" price. The seller of a "call" believes the opposite.

The buyer of a "put" believes that the stock will go down to at least the exercise or "strike" price. And conversely the seller of a "put" doesn't believe that the price of the stock will fall below the "strike" price.

"If at first you don't succeed, try, try again... But then give up. There's no use being a damn fool about it."

Mark Twain

IMPORTANCE OF FUNDAMENTAL ANALYSIS

"The euphoria of a hot market usually results in ignoring marketplace fundamentals."

Keith and Sandi Cunningham

In fundamental analysis of share values, one looks at the details of the company and its financial position. Using financial statements, an analysis takes into consideration the company's revenue, earnings, sales, cash flow, assets, liabilities and expenses. Among other considerations it will look at its outlook for the future. Among the various considerations will be answers to the following questions:

- Is the revenue growing or decreasing?
- Is the company making a profit?
- Can it pay its debts?
- Is management experienced?
- What is the company's ranking among its competitors?
- What is its share of the overall market for its products?
- Is that market growing?

A person may also contact the investor relations department of the company to gather more information.

In the next chapter I delve into pyramid schemes or "Ponzi" schemes, as they are called.

CHAPTER 12

LOWER RISK INVESTING?

Say No to pyramids; RCMP on pyramids; Investment Clubs may not be the answer; Cautions

"The lure of easy money breeds GREED

And the misuse of POWER"

Anonymous

There has been a dearth of pyramid or Ponzi schemes coming to light as of late. Sadly even the perpetrators seem to get away with it due to lax security and competition law enforcement as the CBC news pointed out recently in it's Market Place program. The something for nothing mentality of greed has a strong pull in our society.

SAY NO TO PYRAMIDS

I was my own worst enemy until I learned that money does not grow on trees or fall out of the blue. I was burned several times by pyramid variations before I caught on. How could I have let myself lapse into such greed! Some so called "investment" schemes need to be avoided like the plague.

"Hey, come with me to a Dessert Party. You can make a lot of money!" was how my friend invited me to a woman's gifting group.

I thought why not, it sounds pretty good. A lot of my friends were getting involved. They told me each person contributes $5,000.00 as a gift. When enough people join after me to fill a row of eight people I would rise up one level. Eventually I would rise to the fourth and top level of the pyramid and receive a gift of $40,000.00 from eight contributors. Someone offered information that it had been checked out with the authorities. Because the money gifts were being freely given they said that the Dessert Party was legal.

182

As each of my friends brought other friends, the lowest level filled. More women gave their $5,000.00 disguised as gifts to the person on the highest level. People also introduced more of their friends to join in. As the group enlarged it split into different sections with meetings held at different ladies' homes around the city.

After attending a few meetings the lower row of eight people was filled. Now it was my turn to give a $5,000.00 gift to the lady at the top of my pyramid. The money was supposed to be in $20.00 denominations, be hidden within a gift and be given privately. I heard that ladies had hollowed out loaves of bread to put their money inside. Some hid their gift money in dolls or other things that would not look suspicious.

I was warned to be careful and to make withdrawals from my bank account over a number of days to prevent suspicions. I made several trips to the bank to accumulate two hundred and fifty $20.00 notes. Taking a pumpkin, I hollowed it out and put my gift contribution inside. With the stuffed pumpkin wrapped in fancy patterned cellophane and a large bow, I went to the lady's home one Wednesday afternoon and gave it to her.

Two days later on Friday a news item on TV shocked me. The newsman said that the Police had discovered an illegal Dessert Gifting party. They showed surveillance pictures of one of my friend's homes! The whole scheme immediately collapsed. Several ladies that I didn't know, originators of the scheme, eventually were charged with criminal offences. There was no way to get my money back. The irony was that I was next in line to have been paid but I received nothing.

Of course I had taken the word of others that it was legal without checking it out myself. When the news hit I went on line to the Canadian RCMP information site.

The RCMP description of a pyramid states as follows:

> For the purpose of Section 206(1)(e) of the *Criminal Code* a pyramid scheme is illegal when a person participating in the scheme becomes entitled to receive more money than they invested in the scheme by reason of recruiting others. The money is made through recruitment only, while the product or service has no real value. Schemes of pyramid selling are also prohibited under the Canada's *Competition Act* in Canada.

THAT WAS EXPENSIVE LESSON #1 - $5,000.00 GONE!

The next scheme I tried was in the early days of internet businesses. I was introduced to an internet computer business through a good trusted friend. My friend confirmed to me that it had been checked out by a lady staying with her. She was supposed to have completed all sorts of checking and due diligence. She had even met with one of the up line promoters in Calgary, I was told. Called GMT it was marketing computer affiliate web sites and software.

As people were brought in below by buying the programs their names were added into a matrix. As the numbers of people grew, commissions were paid to the existing participants. From an initial investment of about $200.00 US per share I stood to make a lot of money. Using several accounts, both personal and that of a small private business, I bought 5 shares in GMT. I received a special affiliate web site to bring in more people.

I introduced several friends to the business. For the first several months I received a few checks in small amounts. Then an email arrived to say that the principal involved at the head of GMT had had a stroke. The business was dissolving. More information came saying that another man in the company had already accumulated over a million dollars for himself and wasn't prepared to continue the business. Those of us at the bottom of the pyramid were once again left high and dry.

184

Since I had taken my friend's word that the company was a legitimate business opportunity, I had guaranteed the company to several friends. They had signed up and lost out also so I returned their initial deposit money from my own pocket.

THAT WAS EXPENSIVE LESSON #2 - $ 1,800.00 GONE!

My friend then introduced me to Beacon, an internet training company. It seemed really good. It was selling computer training programs. But it went out of business after I had invested several hundred dollars in it without return.

Then there was Meridian Art to which I was again introduced by a trusted friend. This pyramid scheme sold each participant a piece of art. Then put them into a matrix that was supposed to provide lots of money down the road. I chose my art print picture which I did receive, but the down line that was to have been created beneath me without any of my effort never materialized. Meridian Art also bit the dust with nothing more to show for it.

THESE WERE EXPENSIVE LESSONS #3 & #4 - $414.00 GONE!

By now I realized I had been burned often enough. Several other pyramids were presented to me that I turned down. Several years ago I was invited to attend a "Lady's Investment Club." Since I am an investor I looked forward to meeting and connecting with other women investors. I happened to arrive 15 minutes early for my first meeting. Greeted by the hostess and another early guest I saw a pyramid graph with circles to be filled in with lady's names lying on the table. Seeing the graph I asked whether the investment club was investing in stocks or other types of investments, or whether it was like the gifting club. I was told it was a gifting club but that the goal was only $20,000. Fewer people were needed to reach the goal since they had removed one level.

I said: "When the person who invited me arrives please tell her I did not stay. I lost $5,000.00 in the Dessert Party club. This kind of club is illegal so I will not stay."

 "A lawyer set it up and this one is legal" the hostess replied.

"I think if you check it out with the RCMP you will find it is not legal to expect to receive more money than you put in. When I was involved with a gifting club several people were charged with criminal offences and people arriving at my friend's house were filmed and shown on TV news" I said as I left.

THANKS TO MY PRIOR EXPERIENCE NO EXPENSE BUT MY TIME

"Anything that can't go on forever will end."

Warren Buffet

The next pyramid I was introduced to a year ago was a house building company. It was a slick program with a web page that said that everyone should have a home. It stated that they were providing people with their own homes in just three years. The group purported to be selling prebuilt Styrofoam concrete forms through principals who had run a building company for many years.

They indicated that a participant's commitment was based on the size of home they wanted to receive. Initial down payments of approximately $590.00 for a 1,000 square foot home to $8,600.00 for a home of over 4,000 square feet were required. Then with regular monthly payments and a commitment to bring in one person each month, a participant would purchase pieces of his home. Commissions from bringing in new people were to be paid to offset

186

the monthly payments required by a participant. In theory after your initial buy in you had to pay nothing more.

Several of us at the meeting asked what product we were buying and whether it could be sold to others. We found out that there was no real product, just a promise based on bringing more people into the program. It became obvious to me that this grand plan to house people was yet another pyramid scheme. It depended on bringing in more people at the bottom to fund the people who might eventually gain a house at the top. So once again I said no thanks.

A friend who invested has been receiving regular payments each month even though he did not bring in any members. He has now received more than double what he invested. He said that he was told a former member of the competition bureau had set up the scheme in such a way to avoid the law. Eventually the scheme will have to collapse when no more people are willing to enter the bottom rung.

THANKS TO MY PRIOR EXPERIENCE NO EXPENSE BUT MY TIME

LESSONS LEARNED

- Nothing takes the place of doing your own due diligence before making a decision to invest no matter how much you trust your friend's advice.

- If you have any doubts, check with the authorities before investing, not after.

- Learn the basics of pyramid schemes to spot them and protect yourself.

- When something appears too good to be true it generally is.

- Someone always pays when it collapses. Don't let it be you. Do not participate.

- A participant can be charged with a criminal offence.

INVESTMENT CLUBS MAY NOT BE YOUR ANSWER

On the surface an investment club may seem like a great way for a small investor to make money and learn about investing. An investment club can give an investor an opportunity to earn money through the efforts of the pool of money generated by a group. If it is a small gathering of friends there may be no administration expense but a larger club will definitely have expenses that will get deducted from any profits.

There will be an administration fee to belong to a larger club to offset operating and communicating expenses. The club may offer educational talks and seminars that can be very worthwhile to attend. Along the way the club may expand and offer additional investment vehicles to choose from to participate in. While an investment club may appear attractive there are shortcomings to watch out for.

The club I joined was promoted by a prominent seminar leader. I didn't put much money in to start but later added more. Shares had a three year hold before they could be redeemed. I then joined several of the other offerings the club initiated. The club followed the securities laws and prepared offering memorandums for new investment opportunities. For several years the club seemed to prosper and I made money on my bond issues. They held excellent education seminars that were free to members.

One of the principals put on monthly telephone lectures. Some really great seminars introduced me to excellent business speakers and additional investment opportunities. However, the club expanded far from its initial mandate of investing with membership voting. The principals had changed it into a corporation. Without advising or obtaining agreements of the members the club became a corporation with two principals in control of the shares.

Initially the club put on regular club meetings in several cities with periodic voting on special topics by the membership. Then the club expanded rapidly holding meetings in a number of cities and then into to the United States. Now in addition to selling corporation shares the club was offering a retirement savings fund, insurance, financial planning, two offshoot investment opportunities in Asian countries, several high interest bond issues, real estate land sales and funds, foreclosure funds, etc.

Then word came out that a securities commission had put a halt on some of the club's activities for financial reporting irregularities. The two main principals were fined. The information did not come directly to the club members who only found out through newspaper articles or disclosures on new offerings.

The principal entrepreneur, while being ahead of the markets in many ways kept extolling and opening up new investment ideas. The necessary organizational follow through couldn't keep up. Along with others, a number of family members of the principals were added to the payroll. The staff and office space costs escalated.

Communication about any of these changes was poor or nonexistent. Due to so many vehicles all requiring separate financial reporting, the club's financial statements were many months behind. Being a private corporation there were no legislated requirements to keep the members informed. All education costs were supposed to be self supporting, through public seminar offerings and CD training courses. In fact they were not and were being paid out of the club.

Over the months several additional specialists were added to the payroll. I liked them very much. They were heart people and I felt I could trust them. But after a short period these great people would one after the other no longer be with the club without explanation to the members. Personality conflicts were suspected.

I was caught up in the emotion of greed over easy money. I had invested in several of the real estate fund ventures. One land opportunity was sold to investors far too prematurely. Eventually a year later the club reimbursed me and those that had purchased lots in the not yet approved resort subdivision.

Then a market reversal happened. Many of us began to want to redeem our shares after our three year hold period, but there was no money with which to do so. Regular payments to promissory note holders stopped, thus putting the notes into default. The club's funds were tied up in a number of land ventures etc. that couldn't be easily liquidated.

The club still functions, although has made changes. Certain services are no longer free. Meanwhile one of the principals has moved his family to the United States and has started a new affiliated club there.

"Figures can get manipulated for deception."
Albert Koopman

CAUTIONS:

1. One of the dangers of such a group is that it is a private company or incorporation. Because it's private no legislation protects your interests. In some cases, however, a complaint can be made to a securities commission. Have any such complaints already been laid? Have any of the principals been cited for infractions previously?

190

2. How long has the club been operating? Ask other members whether they are completely satisfied or whether they have problems with any aspect of the club's operations. It can take five years before bad management practices may show up.

3. Check the documents you are required to sign carefully. There will likely be a risk statement to sign whereby you must acknowledge that you are investing in an unsecured risk with possible loss of your funds. Is there an offering memorandum written with full disclosure that would be acceptable to your local securities commission?

4. Under what conditions can you redeem your shares? What is the minimum holding period? How will the club's assets be valued when you ask to redeem your shares? What payment time lag will there be for you to redeem? Can you afford the loss if you receive nothing back?

5. There will ultimately be a cost to pay for any benefits of educational training meetings, telephone talks, and seminars. This cost may be hidden and taken from earned revenues.

6. While the club may have had an initial mandate about how it would operate, a too entrepreneurial leader may expand the operations into too many directions. Each will require separate costly financial reporting and auditing which can greatly reduce the financial returns. The new sidelines may also mean more staffing costs. Those members in the initial club offering may find their club paying for the start up and/or operation of these additional offerings.

7. Often all of the voting control will be in the hands of a few. It is important to do your due diligence on the principals. What is their reputatuion? How trustworthy are they?

8. A tendency toward power and greed by the principals may eventually place your investment in jeopardy. They may assign themselves big salaries. They may take commissions on memberships in addition to large salaries that they appoint for themselves without a membership vote. They may change the timing on rules for redemption of shares to suit themselves. They may pay themselves in share options without approaching the membership. They may use the club's money to pay for personal expenses for travel or hotels.

9. Reporting and communication with the members may be lax. Accounting records may be tardy. Getting information on your investments may not be easily obtained.

10. When you want to redeem your shares there may not be enough money to reimburse you.

Next I look at high risk investing for big bucks.

CHAPTER 13

HIGH RISK INVESTING FOR BIG BUCKS

Risky developments; Resorts can cheat you; Sample subscription agreement

"It won't be the economy that will do in investors; it will be investors themselves"

Warren Buffett

Higher income earnings can be made on private business proposals. These, however, will often not provide the protection of any government overseer. With a greater chance of loss, high risk investing is not for everyone. When you assume the risk involved you must acknowledge that you may never receive your money back. In order to earn higher rates you will likely be required to be an eligible or accredited investor. Different requirements must be met depending on the laws in force in the area you reside in.

FRAUDULENT LAND DEVELOPMENT

Early in my investing experience I had little money to invest, and was a total amateur. I made two bad investments.

The first instance eventually turned out to be fraud. The developer had a nice office and salespeople working for him. It all seemed very legitimate. The development company offered a chance to make big money by buying unit shares in a large land site. The area the land was situated in was growing rapidly at that time. We went out to look at the land and saw the developer's big billboard signs on the site.

Seeing my friends buying in, I bought in without following up on due diligence. When I saw that one of the company's references was the name of a prominent lawyer I knew, I just went along with the deal. My name was registered along with 220 other investors on the title to the land.

At a general meeting the developer showed the investors the site layout design. It incorporated a golf course that was to be part of a residential subdivision. It looked really good. The principal also provided copies of a letter of subdivision approval from the county. Little did we know then that the letter had been falsified.

As time went by the developer, being also the sole trustee, did not pay out the vendor whose land he had bought. The vendor began to foreclose on the site. In addition the Tax Department came after the developer for unpaid tax and GST for unpaid taxes on several properties. This took another huge bite out of the funds. Unknown to us, the developer had used the money paid by the unsuspecting investors to start other projects.

Volunteers formed a group, hired a lawyer, and finally obtained a judgment after several years had passed. The judgment provided return of most of our investment out of the sale of the land after the vendor and government was satisfied. While the land sold for more than what we had paid, all profits that could have been realized went to the Government for unpaid taxes, legal fees and the original vendor.

Some of the investors were never able to be located during the long recovery process. The judge had imposed certain restrictions and holdbacks on the payouts as a result. The judge required country wide advertising to locate missing investors, which was completed without success. It added to the delay for receiving repayment. When funds were released by the court a portion was withheld for the unknown investors. Years later the judge allowed final distribution of the unclaimed remaining proceeds to the investor group.

194

CONDOMINIUM CONVERSION GONE WRONG

Before I realized that the development company was fraudulent, I bought into a second one of their schemes. The developer provided a proposal for a condominium apartment conversion and sale. Their initial proforma for the conversion proposal indicated a 67% return to the investors. Using my experience of building management I reworked the numbers and came up with a potential of 27% return which I thought was more realistic.

I toured the apartment building which was legally a condominium but had only been rented to date. It seemed to have good potential so I bought in. My interest was once again registered on title.

Soon the group of investors realized the developer, as sole trustee again, had added another mortgage to the title. This second mortgage was placed with one of his own companies. With legal help the investors began the process to take over. Again a working committee had to be formed, a lawyer hired, a corporation created, and decisions made. I spent many hours as a director and secretary. I took many trips out of town to meet with other investors while we worked to get the property cleared.

As the only local investor director with condominium management experience, I oversaw roof replacement, carpet installation, painting and furnishing of the common areas. I had replacement bylaws written, prepared a condominium budget, ordered a reserve study and made a reserve spending plan.

Several board members and I renegotiated with the original mortgage lender bank to allow us to pay off their mortgage in increments. This was necessary to allow individual sales of units. These tasks were all required in order to begin marketing.

Following several presentations the committee selected a Realtor. He began selling units as each was vacated, cleaned and painted. Unfortunately he was only a listing Realtor, and did not honor his detailed agreement. We then hired a different Realtor and real estate company. This time the investors successfully sold the condominium units without loss, each of us even realizing a small gain.

Many small investors lost money through this one developer's schemes. Unfortunately the Security Commission never charged him. The RCMP did finally begin an investigation. I supplied a lot of evidence but never heard anything after that. We also discovered that two lawyers working for the developer seemed to be in on the fraud.

Fraud is not always easy to spot. He fooled us for several years and sadly he is still at large five years later.

CAUTIONS:

1. Do not take the advice of friends without doing your own due diligence.

2. What is the history behind the company and the principal?

3. How long have they been in business?

4. Have the securities commission received any complaints against the principal?

5. Who else can you check with before investing?
    The county where the development is to be?
    The accounting firm?

6. Check the lawyers' reputation - Find out if he is indeed representing them.

7. Get a copy of the land title
   Check for encumbrances.

   Are any mortgages in good standing?

8. Are there any unpaid property taxes? Or federal taxes like GST on land sales?

9. Who is the trustee for the unit holder owners?

   Is it a Trust company or the principal?

10. What abilities under your agreement does the trustee have?

11. Which activities are the trustee restricted from performing without a vote of the unit holders?

12. Ask your lawyer to review the documents for protective clauses to add before you sign.

13. Does the proposed profit look excessive? Question it. Is it time to walk away?

14. Don't accept and believe promises of easy money to come in a few years.

"Fraud is deceit.

The essence of fraud is I create trust in you and then I betray that trust and get you to give me something of value."

William K. Black

RESORT DEVELOPMENTS CAN CHEAT YOU

*"Like the loyal wife betrayed by her husband, shareholders
are often the last to know about problems - and by the time
they find out, it is usually too late."*

Albert Koopman

Along with seven hundred people I attended a high powered
investment seminar. A line up of investment opportunities was
introduced by the principal organizer. One of the presenters, who
seemed to be a very nice open person, was selling shares in his five
star resort in the Dominican Republic.

The brochure pictures looked elegant and lovely. In order to make a
referral commission fee, the seminar organizer was offering free stays
at the resort. I accepted the opportunity and went with a friend to
enjoy a holiday there.

The site was gorgeous. It cascaded down a hillside with a number of
swimming pools on different elevations. Luxury hotel rooms were
located in various separate buildings placed throughout the site. Each
was encircled with gardens and close to one of a number of pools.
The beach area and two of the five on-site restaurants were located at
the tip of the property on the ocean. There was a tourist attraction
nearby called Ocean World, which was under construction. Friendly
and cordial staff made us feel welcome.

After being there a few days I was approached about investing in the
company. The salesman told me of plans to add a spa and
condominium units. I could really see the potential that the
beautiful all inclusive resort offered. Especially appealing was the
proximity to Ocean World and the plans being built there. The
salesman indicated that the funds would be safe as they were being
invested in a company registered in an off shore account in Turks
and Caicos.

I was emotionally smitten with the resort. Investing a little less than their minimum amount of $10,000.00 a share I looked forward to receiving nice earnings some day.

A glossy newsletter would arrive at least once a year along with financial information. Each year the financial statements always indicated that expenses were higher than the revenue. There always seemed to be further development plans that would expand the resort. So there were never any payments on my shares. At least each year the resort would hold at reduced rates a special shareholder's seminar.

In one of the years the resort bought out several adjacent homes and apartment buildings. In another year they now had a yacht that they would rent out. I was willing to wait for a return on my investment because I believed in the principals and their business knowledge.

When I went down for a second visit several years later the spa was now in place and new high end condominiums were being marketed.

There always seemed to be new offerings being promoted on each of my visits. While I declined, friends I met there decided to invest in this newest offering of the resort group.

The expansion developments were always costly. I assumed they were the reason why the shareholders were not receiving any benefits.

A few years went by, and the principal owners of the resort had now added a new separate venture in another area of the island. I received a call from my investor friend. He said that their interest had been switched to another complex and that his payment method was now not what they had believed they were buying.

Finally I received word from a newspaper article that the whole resort group was a Ponzi (pyramid) scheme. There was apparently a class action lawsuit for recovery of funds in process against the principals. Yet again my tax accountant wrote off my share interest as a capital loss.

Once again I had made an assumption that the original seminar organizer had done due diligence on all presenters and their companies. I assumed the participating offerings had been checked out and were above board. I had done no due diligence myself. Perhaps the principals had even operated legitimately in the beginning. In which case a more thorough due diligence before hand may not have disclosed the true situation. But at least I would have known more about the backgrounds of the principals and something about the investment and any future plans for growth.

CAUTIONS:

1. Don't assume the conference presenter has verified the honesty of the presenters. In many cases the presenting organization makes a commission on all sales made at a conference.

2. Don't be fooled like I was by a feeling that the presenter is a really nice fellow. Nice people can do bad things. Do your due diligence on the presenter's history.

3. How long has the selling organization been doing business? Can you obtain a company financial statement? Are you able to contact references?

4. Check into the resort region. How popular is it? Is there really a market there? Are sales of properties brisk or very slow?

5. Don't let yourself be stampeded into singing in a hurry. Have your lawyer review any documents that you need to sign.

6. Was there a risk statement to sign? Did you receive an offering memorandum that provided complete details of the proposed plans as well as about the interests of the principals?

7. Do you realize that getting your income from a foreign company may not be easy? There may also be tax implications.

Other opportunities are reviewed in the next chapter.

Sample forms follow:

SAMPLE SUBSCRIPTION AGREEMENT
XXX MANAGEMENT INC.

SERIES "A" DEBENTURES – SUBSCRIPTION AGREEMENT

THIS SUBSCRIPTION AGREEMENT is made the _____day of
_____, 20__,

BETWEEN:

Name:

_____

Address:

_____

Email address:

_____

Social Insurance Number(SIN):_____

(the "Purchaser")

AND:

XXX MANAGEMENT INC., An Alberta Company
with its registered office at
_____Calgary AB _____

(the "Company")

WITNESSES THAT WHEREAS the Purchaser wishes to purchase
Series A Debentures (the "Debentures") in the principal amount of $
_____ (the "Principal Amount") from the Company, subject to
this Agreement and to the Trust Deed dated for reference November
13th, 2008 made by the Company in favour of XYZ Trust company
as Trustee (the "Trust Deed");

NOW THEREFORE IN CONSIDERATION of the agreements contained herein and other good and valuable consideration, the parties covenant and agree as follows:

1. SUBSCRIPTION, PURPOSE and TERMS

1. **Subscription:** Subject to the other provisions herein, the Purchaser hereby subscribes for the Principal Amount of Debentures for a price equal to the Principal Amount (the "Subscription Price"), and agrees to pay the Subscription Price to the Company.

2. **Purpose:** The Company shall use the Subscription Price for the purposes required and permitted by the Trust Deed.

3. **Closing:** On receipt of the Subscription Price, the Company will cause the Debentures to be issued and the certificate representing such Debentures to be delivered to the Purchaser.

4. **Terms of Debentures:** The Debentures shall be on the terms set forth in Schedule A hereto, shall be in the form of Schedule B hereto, and shall be issued under the terms of the Trust Deed.

2. MISCELLANEOUS

a. This is the entire agreement regarding the Purchaser's loan to the Company, and supersedes any prior agreement relating to the same loan. The Company has made no representation or warranty to the Purchaser except as set out herein.

b. In the event of any conflict between the terms of this Agreement and the terms of any Trust Deed, the terms of the Trust Deed shall govern.

c. The Company may not assign or transfer its obligations hereunder. The Purchaser may not assign or transfer its rights hereunder without the prior written consent of the Company, which may be withheld by the Company without giving any reason.

d. This Agreement shall be construed and enforced in accordance with, and the rights of the parties shall be governed by, the laws of British Columbia. All disputes hereunder will be referred to British Columbia Courts. The parties irrevocably submit to the non-exclusive jurisdiction of British Columbia Courts.

e. This Agreement may be executed in counterparts and by facsimile transmission and such counterparts and facsimile transmissions together shall form one and the same instrument.

f. In this Agreement:

  i. unless there is something in the subject matter or the context necessarily inconsistent therewith, expressions defined in the Trust Deed shall have the meaning set forth therein;

  ii. where the context requires, references to the singular shall be deemed to include the plural, references to the masculine shall be deemed to include the feminine and neuter genders and a body corporate, and vice versa; and

  iii. headings form no part of this Agreement and shall be deemed to have been inserted for convenience of reference only.

IN WITNESS WHEREOF the parties have executed this Agreement.

SIGNED, SEALED AND DELIVERED
by the Purchaser in the presence of:

_____   _____

Signature of Witness   Purchaser Signature

_____   _____

Print Witness Name   Purchaser Name

_____

Witness Address

XXX   MANAGEMENT INC.

_____

by its authorized signatory

SAMPLE SUBSCRITION AGREEMENT
SCHEDULE A
TERM SHEET: XXX   Management Inc. Series A Debentures

Interest	<u>1.5%</u> per month (18% per annum) payable 1st of each month, in arrears.
Term & Maturity Date	____years commencing from receipt of subscription fund.
Redemption	Redeemable at the instance of the Company in whole or in part at any time. Redemption price is principal plus accrued interest.
Security	Security interest in all assets and undertaking of the Company (as set out in Trust Deed).
Ranking	Debentures of all series rank pari passu, and subordinate to security granted for Vendor Financing (see Trust Deed). Replacement debt for Vendor Financing will also rank pari passu. Additional debt may be granted priority in accordance with the Trust Deed, but only after replacement of the Vendor Financing.
Events of Default	1) default in payment of principal and interest, not cured after 45 days notice
	2) breach of representation and warranty
	3) breach of covenant not cured for 60 days after notice
	4) Company applies for a Receiver, fails to pay debts generally, commits act of bankruptcy, or institutes proceedings in bankruptcy; is adjudged bankrupt, liquidated or dissolved, or a Receiver is appointed
	5) judgement is taken against the Company for $100,000 and not released or satisfied for 60 days
	6) Trust Deed or Debentures are held unenforceable
	7) Vendor enforces security on any default under Vendor Financing
Acceleration and Enforcement	Trustee may accelerate with consent of Holders of 25% (by value) of debentures; that decision may be reversed if approved by 66 2/3% of Holders. Trustee may take enforcement action with approval of 66 2/3% of Holders
Holder's Approval	Holders of debentures can make certain amendments to the Trust Deed, agree to grant priority, and take certain other actions binding all Holders, by Extraordinary Resolution (defined in the Trust Deed). Quorum for Holders' meetings is 50% (by value) of all debentures, plus $1. Proxy voting is permitted.

SCHEDULE B
FORM OF DEBENTURE

Unless this certificate is presented to XXX Management Inc. and its consent is obtained for any transfer, any transfer, pledge or other use hereof for value or otherwise by or to any person is wrongful, null and void.

This debenture is not transferable in the Province of Alberta except pursuant to an exemption from the prospectus requirements contained in applicable securities legislation.

In addition, this debenture may be subject to restrictions on transfer under the provisions of securities legislation where the registered holder is resident.

No._____

Principal Sum: $ _____

Issue Date: _____

Maturity Date: _____

Interest Rate: _____

XXX MANAGEMENT INC.

(Incorporated under the laws of Alberta)

SERIES A DEBENTURE

XXX MANAGEMENT INC. (herein called the "Company") for value received hereby acknowledges itself indebted to and promises to pay to _____ the Principal Sum set out above ("Principal Sum") in lawful money of Canada, and to pay interest from the Issue Date set out above ("Issue Date") in like money on the Principal Sum from time to time outstanding at the Interest Rate per annum set out above ("Interest Rate") calculated monthly and payable on the 1st day of each month during the term for the previous month with the principal sum payable in full on the Maturity Date set out above ("Maturity Date") and, should the Company default in payment of any principal or interest payable hereunder, to pay interest both before and after default and judgment on the amount in default at the Interest Rate, calculated and payable on the same dates.

This is one of the Series A Debentures of the Debentures ("Debentures") of the Company issued and to be issued and secured under a Deed of Trust with all amendments and supplements thereto made or entered into from time to time in accordance with its terms (the "Trust Deed") dated for reference November 13, 2008 and made between the Company and XYZ Trust Company (who, and whose successors in the trust, are called the "Trustee").

The Trust Deed describes, _inter alia_, the security interest and floating charge by which this Debenture is secured and the properties thereby mortgaged and charged; the nature and extent of the security; the provisions as to appropriation of the proceeds from realization of the security as among series of Debentures; the rights of holders of Debentures, the Company and the Trustee; provisions for meetings of holders and rendering resolutions passed at such meetings and instruments in writing signed by the holders of a specified majority of Debentures outstanding binding on all holders, subject to the provisions of the Trust Deed; requirements for issue of additional Debentures and other series of Debentures; and all terms and conditions upon which

Debentures are, and are to be, issued and secured and to which they are subject, to all of which terms and conditions the holder of this Debenture assents and shall be subject.

If an Event of Default (defined in the Trust Deed) occurs, the principal of and all interest accrued and unpaid on all Debentures at any such time outstanding under the Trust Deed may be declared and become due and payable under the conditions, in the manner and with the effect provided in the Trust Deed.

This Debenture is redeemable in whole at any time or in part from time to time at the option of the Company in accordance with the terms and conditions of the Trust Deed.

The Company and the Trustee may deem and treat the Person in whose name this Debenture is registered as the absolute owner of this Debenture for the purpose of receiving payment of or on account of the principal hereof and interest due hereon and for all purposes whatsoever and the Company and the Trustee shall not be affected by any notice to the contrary.

IN WITNESS WHEREOF XXX Management Inc. has caused this Debenture to be signed by its duly authorized officer as of the Issue Date.

XXX MANAGEMENT INC.

Per:_____

CANADIAN ACCREDITED INVESTOR DEFINITION

Accredited Investor - (defined in NI 45-106) means:

(a) an individual who, either alone or with a spouse, beneficially owns, directly or indirectly, financial assets having an aggregate realizable value that before tax ~ but net of any related liabilities, exceeds $1,000,000;

(b) an individual whose net income before taxes exceeded $200,000 in each of the 2 most recent calendar years or whose net income before taxes combined with that of a spouse exceeded $300,000 in each of the 2 most recent calendar years and who, in either case, reasonably expects to exceed that net income level in the current calendar year;

(d) a person, other than an individual or investment fund, that has net assets of at least $5,000,000 as shown on its most recently prepared financial statements;

(e) a person in respect of which all of the owners of interests, direct, indirect or beneficial except the voting securities required by law to be owned by directors, are persons that are accredited investors;

(g) the Business Development Bank of Canada incorporated under the Business Development Bank of Canada Act (Canada);

(h) a subsidiary of any person referred to in paragraphs (1) or (g). if the person owns all of the voting securities of the subsidiary~ except the voting securities required by law to be owned by directors of that subsidiary;

(i) a person registered under the securities legislation of a jurisdiction of Canada as an adviser or dealer, other than a person registered solely as a limited market dealer under one or both of the Securities Act (Ontario) or the Securities Act (Newfoundland and Labrador);

(j) an individual registered or formerly registered

under the securities legislation of a jurisdiction of Canada as
a representative of a person referred. to in paragraph
(i);

(k) the Government of Canada or a jurisdiction of Canada, or
any crown Corporation, agency or wholly owned entity of the
Government of Canada or a jurisdiction of Canada;

(1) a municipality, public board or commission in Canada and
a metropolitan community, school board, the Comite de
gestion de la taxe scolaire de l'ile de Montreal or an
intermunicipal management board in Quebec;

(m) any national, federal, state, provincial, territorial or
municipal government of or in any foreign   jurisdiction,
or any agency of that government;

(n) a pension fund that is regulated by either 1he Office of the
Superintendent of Financial Institutions (Canada) or a pension
commission or similar regulatory authority~ of a jurisdiction
of Canada;

(o) an investment fund that distributes or has distributed its securitie
only to

  (i) a person that is or was an accredited investor at the time
  of distribution;

  (ii) a person that acquires or acquired securities in the circumstances
  referred to in Sections 2.10 (.Minimumamount investment], and
  2.19 [Additional investment in investment funds] of NI 45-106; OR

  (iii) a person described in paragraph (I) or (ii) that acquires only to or
  acquired securities under Section 2.1 g Investment fund reinvestment]
  of NI 45-1 06~

(p) an investment fund that distributes or has distributed securities
under a prospectus in a jurisdiction of Canada for which the
regulator or, in

Quebec, the securities regulatory authority, has issued a receipt;

(q) a trust company or trust corporation registered or authorized to carry on business under the Trust and Loan Companies Act (Canada) or under comparable legislation in a jurisdiction of Canada or a foreign jurisdiction, acting on behalf of a fully managed account managed by the trust company or trust corporation, as the case may be;

(r) a person acting on behalf of a fully managed account managed by that person, if that person

(i) is registered or authorized to carry on business as an adviser or the equivalent under the securities legislation of a jurisdiction of Canada or a foreign jurisdiction; and

(ii) in Ontario. is purchasing a security that is not a security of au investment fund;

(s) a registered charity under the Income Tax Act (Canada) that, in regard to the trade, has obtained advice from an eligibility adviser or an adviser registered under the securities legislation of the jurisdiction of the registered charity to give advice on the securities being traded;

(t) an entity organized in a foreign jurisdiction that is analogous to any of the entities referred to in paragraphs (f) to (i) or paragraph (n) in form and function;

(u) an investment fund that is advised by a person registered as an adviser or a person that is exempt from registration as an adviser; OR

(v) a person that is recognized or designated by the securities regulatory authority or, except in Ontario and Quebec, the regulator as

(i) an accredited investor; or

(ii) an exempt purchaser in Alberta or British Columbia

(ii) an exempt purchaser in Alberta or British Columbia

after NI 45-106 comes into force;

and for purposes hereof: words and phrases which are used in this Accredited Investor Certificate and which are defined in NI 45-106 shall have the meaning ascribed thereto in NI 45-106.

CHAPTER 14

OTHER OPPORTUNITIES TO CHECK INTO

High Interest paying developments; Colored diamonds are costly;
Mortgage funds; Loan corporation bonds pay;
Other opportunities I bypassed.

"Risk comes from not knowing what you are doing"

Warren Buffett

HIGH INTEREST PAYING DEVELOPMENTS

When a company is willing to pay high interest rates to secure money for a construction project it will likely be because conventional financing is not available. Again of critical importance will be the due diligence you complete on the principals and the construction company's current financial position. Do not rely on news articles or a glossy web site or presentation meeting.

If I had investigated the principals in a development scheme in Canmore, Alberta I would not now be paying my share of legal fees and receivership fees on a collapsed development investment. I was lured by an interest rate of 14% paid quarterly. Apparently the principals had other failures beneath their belt and were not considered trustworthy had I only checked beforehand. Brochures showed photographs of the complex that was already half completed. The company's web site and several news articles from the Calgary Herald led me to believe it was a genuine investment in a successful company that had completed other projects. Later I went to see the construction site and was impressed with the look of the buildings. I didn't realize that they had been grossly overvalued and that no actual construction work had been done for several years. In fact I recently learned that the City of Canmore was considering bulldozing them down since the site was inactive and had past their agreed upon completion date.

The investor group I am part of is holding a fifteen million dollar mortgage on the property. When we complete the legal takeover and finish construction of the project I suspect that I may end up with 25 cents on the dollar for my $100,000.00 invested. That is if I am lucky. I will also have to wait several more years for the construction to be completed and units in the complex to be sold.

CAUTIONS:

1. The offering of higher interest rates mean there will be greater risk of loss. Due diligence is imperative. Have your lawyer review all documentation before you sign anything.

2. Often development companies will incorporate a separate entity under which to build the project. Through thus limiting their liability in case of failure they do not jeopardize their parent company.

3. If the development runs out of funds it will be hard to get all the investors to agree to a course of action. Make certain that the initial papers drawn up for you to sign have foreseen this outcome and provided a plan of action for it.

4. Being registered on title is no protection from loss. However being registered in first position as a mortgage holder is better than registration in second position as a second mortgage holder.

5. If one person is the trustee he or she may make decisions that affect you without your knowledge. It is better to have a registered trust company be the trustee.

6. You may be able to take part in a large project with less money invested. Market conditions can change causing the development to run out of funding. You may find you are one of 150 or more people who now must determine a course of action to recover their money. Whether through

foreclosure, bankruptcy or other means, contacting the other investors and getting majority agreement is not easy. More of your money will be needed to pay for insurance, security, and lawyers.

7. You may need to take responsibility to volunteer your time to act on a committee on behalf of the investor group. It can take years for a bankruptcy or a case of fraud to be completed through the courts and eventual sale. You may be lucky to get back cents on the dollar.

COLOURED DIAMONDS ARE COSTLY

Through an investment club I was caught up in the idea of purchasing wholesale a fancy colored diamond. I was told of the rapid appreciation in value of fancy colored diamonds. This was occurring because of reducing availability of supply. The rare red, red orange and red purple stones come only from one Rio Tinto mine in Australia. These colors are becoming much harder to find.

Wholesale prices of the smallest stones began at $25,000.00 each. Looking to diversify my investments I invested in a rare colored diamond which I left in the vault of the diamond dealer. I learned that a colored diamond investment is meant to be held for at least five years in order to appreciate in value sufficiently to provide a return on the investment.

Even though my stone is small it is engraved with an identification number from Rio Tinto. It came with a Gemologist Institute certificate and insurance certificate from Lloyd's of London.

TIP

My diamond is still being held by the diamond company. But it would be prudent to take possession of your stone and keep it in your own safety deposit box. If the firm I purchased from were not honest they might sell the same diamond to a number of people sending each person copies of the certificates.

EXPENSIVE LESSON:

It never occurred to me to check how much it would cost me to sell the stone later. I learned to my sorrow after I purchased that the selling commission with the broker is fifty percent of the selling cost. My stone would have to increase 100% in value just to give me back my initial money invested.

I have experienced that the next three investments topics discussed have provided regular sustainable income at higher rates of interest.

MORTGAGE INVESTMENT FUNDS PAY

"When opportunity knocks, open the door."
Albert J. Lowry & Richard C, Powelson

While perhaps not attractive at present due to difficult real estate market conditions, money held in long established mortgage funds has provided me steady monthly income. These funds do not pay the higher risk rates of 13% to 24% interest that some more risky investments may pay. Mortgage funds can pay at dependable steady rates of 8% to 10% annually. The key to a safer mortgage fund investment is the level of equity that the fund maintains in its portfolio. 35% equity to overall appraised value of the property that their mortgages are placed on can provide dependable returns. The fund will take about 1.5 to 2% in fees before paying out 8% to 10%.

These investment vehicles are offered as first or second mortgage funds or blended first and second mortgage funds. One may elect to receive monthly payments or elect to let the interest compound providing an even greater earning rate over a number of years.

CAUTIONS:

1. Check investment fund references carefully.

2. How long have they been in business?

3. What protection do you have for your investment?

4. What is their loan to value lending ratio?

5. How many mortgages are in their portfolio?

6. Can you obtain client references?

7. What notice period is required to redeem your shares?

COMMERCIAL STRIP MALLS

Certain development firms offer the smaller investor an opportunity to own a partnership share in an existing commercial building or shopping mall. The developer acquires the existing commercial real estate in a growing market or an area that still retains potential. They complete the due diligence, make a purchase offer, arrange the financing, and arrange the legal work. A limited partnership to hold the property is formed. The developer company remains as trustee to operate the mall or building for a management fee.

The sales of units will be restricted to accredited investors. Partnership shares will be offered to investors starting at $10,000.00 or $25,000.00 per unit. The acquisition value of a mall may be anywhere from $6,000,000.00 to $25,000,000.00. Therefore there could be five hundred or more investors that will own partnership units in one shopping mall.

The developer allows a period of time to sell the units prior to taking possession of the property on December 1st. By taking possession of the complex on December 1st and accumulating all of the start up costs into one month, the developer is able to pass on to the investor partners a substantial tax deduction for the first part year. This can be written off against other earnings for that year.

From the date of purchase of a partnership until possession the developer pays a small rate of interest on your advanced funds. In addition to the tax deduction the investor receives quarterly distributions of the net mall rental proceeds.

By the fifth year the property will be refinanced to return the equity portion of the investment back to the partnership members. The exit plan is to either continue ownership of the mall after five years or sell the complex.

The combination of tax savings, earnings and equity growth can provide a return of 12% to 14% annually on invested capital. Once your equity has been returned your earnings will continue until the investor group sells the mall.

The negative factor is that you are at the mercy of the majority when it comes to the five year decision point. A majority vote will decide whether to sell or to refinance the property. Under certain conditions one can offer their interest in the property for sale if necessary between terms.

CAUTIONS:

1. How long has the developer been in business?

2. How reliable have been their earning forecasts?

3. Can you obtain client references?

4. Review the conditions carefully in the subscription agreement

5. What kind of exterior finishes are there on the buildings?

6. What regular maintenance will be required?

7. What is the condition of the roof?

8. What is the condition of the parking area?

9. What are the types of businesses renting spaces?

10. Is there a good anchor tenant like a bank that draws people there regularly?

11. What type of leases are the tenants on?

12. Are there common area costs that the partnership will have to pay?

13. Is the mall easily accessible and visible to traffic?

14. Project ahead five years - Will this mall still be needed to serve the area?

15. What are the terms under which the mall may be sold or refinanced?

16. Additional capital contributions could be required in future.

17. Can you resell your unit to someone else?

18. What are your voting rights?

19. How often will there be meetings of the partnership unit holders?

LOAN CORPORATION BONDS PAY

Good, albeit high risk investments can be made in companies in the lending business. They may pay much higher rates of return depending on their length of time in business and their track record. Your only collateral, however, will be a bond certificate. You will be relying on the loan company's good reputation and good business practices. Generally as private companies, operating internet loan services with few tangible assets, they are considered very high risk investments. As a result the rates they pay may run from 12% to 24% per annum.

CAUTIONS:

1. Do thorough due diligence on the company and the principals.

2. How long have they been in business?

3. Can you receive references from their clients?

4. Do they send regular communications to their investors?

5. Who do they provide the funds to? Do they operate their own outlets?

6. Are the rates being charged for use of the money they loan in accordance with usury laws?

7. Are there any outstanding legal claims against the company?

OTHER OPPORTUNITIES MAY NOT BE ALL THEY ARE CRACKED UP TO BE

I looked into several opportunities where an investor would own **BANK DEBIT TERMINALS**. One firm was supplying these to taxi companies. In one case the investor would receive regular monthly payments. However, the money being returned in the first five years was only return of the investor's capital. No earnings would be received until after the fifth year. The company did include the upgrade to the new equipment as technical improvement required.

I bought a course and for a while I tried to work on **U. S. TAX LIENS AND DEEDS.** These are opportunities to advance the U.S. county or state money to pay the taxes on a delinquent property. If the owner repays the money to the county the investor receives his money back as well as earning the set interest rate. Every county or state pays a different interest rate.

Tax lien lots are offered at auctions and afterward through counter sales. Tax liens or deeds are not easily acquired unless one can attend the tax auctions. You need to do due diligence on the properties you plan to bid on prior to the auction. This is necessary to avoid obtaining a property that has environmental or other expensive problems. I found it was not so easy to do tax lien work at a distance.

The chance of gaining a property for unpaid taxes is very slim. In normal circumstances, most tax liens get paid back. Thus you may earn only the interest. Each also has different redemption rules. It may take several years to resolve whether you can get ownership of the property. During which time you will have to pay the taxes again for the second year.

Becoming an **E-BAY SELLER** was also investigated. In this type of venture you contract with a wholesaler to market his products for a fee. You make the sales through E-Bay and the wholesaler does the shipping for you. This would involve a certain time commitment and computer time. This type of involvement did not interest me but others have done well at it.

Buying **FORECLOSURE HOMES** in various locations in the U.S. was another opportunity. Two different companies offered similar packages. One of them did much more due diligence than the other to determine marketable areas to invest in.

These companies would buy groups of foreclosed homes at very low prices from the banks. They would then offer them to investors at prices presumably much lower than the appraised value. Some were offered at $18,000.00 that were said to appraise at $45,000.00 or more.

The investor would buy the home along with a management service package. The management company would try to either sell the home as is or rent it for a decent cash flow. The homes would be sold to new owners with very low down payments and an affordable mortgage at a good interest rate. The mortgage payments would be set less than a comparable house would rent for. This would attract purchasers.

Many of the homes offered were generally run down or even damaged. They were being sold as is to purchasers. Investors were given a guarantee that the company would find a buyer within six months. In the meantime there would be carrying and closing costs to pay. The service agreement offered was only for one year.

I elected not to get involved. I felt there was insufficient protection for myself to become an absentee landlord at such a distance. In the event there were problems the homes could have required travelling to make necessary arrangements for collections or repairs, etc. Some of the houses also did not appraise well. In addition there would have been withholding taxes to pay on a U.S. investment since I am Canadian

Canadian purchasers of US foreclosure homes discovered that American laws prohibit Canadians from making any of their own property repairs and that complying with certain US tax laws eat into their rental or sale profit.

CAUTIONS:

1. Do your due diligence on the principals and the company.

2. Is the home in an area with good continuing potential value?

3. Do the proposal numbers make economical sense?

4. Do they fit your goals and personality?

5. Do you want to do any marketing, sales or other work necessary yourself?

6. If not, how do you plan to manage the sale or rental?

7. Can you obtain written appraisals of the actual value in order to determine whether a purchase would be worth while?

8. How will the tax implications affect you?

9. Are there any other requirements such as registrations or licenses that you will be required to obtain?

AFTERWARD

"Unfortunately the reason most people are not rich is because they are terrified of losing."

Robert T. Kiyosaki

"Losers avoid failing. And failure turns losers into winners."

Robert T. Kiyosaki

By now I hope you have had a good laugh at my follies. I made so many mistakes!

While I made numerous mistakes through being inadequately informed, due to the fact that I did not do sufficient due diligence in advance of my purchases, I still managed to have many successes.

This book has provided you with the benefit of my investment mistakes. They are reminders of what not to do, followed by lists of what to do. You may want to use this book as a reference guide when you are planning new investments.

THE KEY

The key to successful investing is knowledge.

Do your due diligence first.

Only then put your money down.

- Do your due diligence. Due diligence. I cannot emphasize due diligence enough.
- Do not let the lure of easy money blind you.
- Being a careless investor can cost you money.
- Being a high risk taker can cost you plenty.

- Set your emotions aside.
- Make no decisions while caught up in emotional responses to great sounding deals.
- Give yourself a cooling off period before signing anything.
- Nothing is more important than looking before you leap into any kind of investment.
- If your investigation means that you miss an opportunity, there will always be another one to put money into.
- Learn all that you can before signing over your hard earned funds.

You will find great resources through books, the internet, and specialty training or networking groups. You may also want to seek out experienced mentors to guide you.

Save yourself tears and despair. Pay heed to the voice of experience.

May your money tree grow and provide overflowing abundance.

BIBLIOGRAHY

DUE DILIGENCE IS A MUST

John Tansowny has written a great course on Due Diligence. It teaches you the steps to follow to find out about a company before you invest. With adequate due diligence you need not make the mistakes that I did. Contact thecorporatecoach@live.com for purchase information.

The Art of Due Diligence course by John Tansowny is also available from the Freedom Investment club. Their web site is www.FICinvestors.com

STOCK TRADING TOOLS

Investools web site is www.investools.com. They offer training and a software system to use for selecting stocks.

5-Point Star Trader Program by Quantum Vision Inc. is a training course teaching various methods of how to trade in the stock market. (800) 956-0656 website: www.StockMarketWorkshop.com

7 Keys to Financial Enlightenment course is available from www.FICinvestors.com.

James Dines – puts out an investment newsletter every three weeks. His book aids understanding of how fear and greed affect the market and what to watch for. It is titled *"How to Make Money using MASS PSYCHOLOGY"* ISBN - 0-9649689-0-8

BUSINESS TRAINING HELPS

T. Harvy Eker's organization **Peak Potentials** holds business training and investment courses. They put on Millionaire Mind, Millionaire School and Guerilla Business School among a number of other courses. One of Harv Eker's books is *"Secrets of the Millionaire Mind"* ISBN 0-06-076329-0 His web site is www.peakpotentials.com

Bill Bartmann teaches Billionaire Secrets to Success. His follow up courses can help anyone get a great start in their chosen business. He also teaches how to make money buying bad loans. His book *"Billionaire Secrets to Success"* is excellent. ISBN: 1-933285-31-1 His newest book is *"Bail Out Riches, How everyday Investors can Make a Fortune Buying Bad Loans for Pennies on the Dollar"* His web site is www.billbartmann.com

Robert Kiyosaki and his associates teach people to be millionaires. One of his books is: *"Rich Dad Poor Dad. What the Rich Teach Their kids about Money - What the Poor and Middle Class do Not"* ISBN 0-9643856-1-9Pbk

His training board games are fun to play while you learn. "Cashflow 101" teaches basic investment. "Cashflow 202" teaches options trading

Other books and courses *"Rich Dad's Cash Flow Quadrant"* Rich Dad's Guide to Investing; Rich Dad's Rich Kid Smart Kid; Rich Dad's Retire Young Retire Rich
Rich Dad's Prophecy; Rich Dad's Success Stories; Rich Dad's Guide to Becoming Rich Without Cutting Up Your Credit Cards; Rich Dad's Who Took My Money; Rich Dad Poor Dad for Teens; Rich Dad's Escape from the Rat Race; Rich Dad's Before You Quit Your Job

Other products are available on his web site www.richdad.com

FIC Investment Corp. produces teleseminars, newsletters and holds classes on investment, real estate, buying foreclosures and stock market investing. They host an investment conference called

Investfest where you can meet great trainers as well as receive investment opportunities.

LANDLORDING LESSONS

Wright J. Thurston puts on seminars and sells a number of landlording books, courses and forms. "*7 Step Checklist for successful real Estate Investing*" Other CD course and books are available on the internet.

Tim Johnston – Pro-Active Landlording booklet by Tim Johnson and Don Campbell and CD information may still be available through Don Campbell and R.E.I.N.

REAL ESTATE GURUS

Raymond Aaron Group teaches real estate and goal setting courses. Raymond's web site is www.aaron.com

R.E.I.N. (The Real Estate Investment Network) led by Don Campbell

holds regular meetings in several cities and provides excellent landlord training courses. Their "Quick Start" program is excellent. www.reincanada.com

Ozzie Jurock holds real estate courses, provides advice and publishes a newsletter. His web site is www.ozziejurock.com

Robert G. Allen teaches classes and has several books about buying real estate with little or no money down. His books are: "*No Money Down*" "*Creating Wealth*" ISBN 0-671-44281-3 "*Multiple Streams of Income*" and others. His web site is www.robertgallen.com

Mr. Albert J. Lawry's books are: *"How to Become Financially Independent Buying Real Estate,"* ISBN 1-881554-08-2 and *"Formulas for Wealth, How to Create a Fortune in Real Estate"* by Albert J. Lowry and Richard C. Powelson.

Ron LeGrand holds real estate training camps and has CD courses available. His web site is www.ronlegrand.com

FINANCE KNOWLEDGE

Mary Buffet and David Clark have authored three books: *"Tao of Warren Buffet"*, ISBN -13:978-1-4165-4132-5 *"Buffettology"*, and an excellent book called *"Warren Buffet and the Interpretation of Financial Statements"* by Mary Buffett and David Clark It is the best financial guide I have found. ISBN – 13-978-1-4165-7318-0

Keith Cunningham teaches finance with his Keys to the Vault program. His web site is www.keystothe vault.com

GREAT COACHES

Shellie Ann Hunt of Success is By Design is a great empowering personal and business development coach. Her web sites are www.successisbydesign.com and www.whitesagemedia.com

Andrew Barber Starkey is a master coach who teaches goal setting as well as personal and business development. His web site is www.procoachsystem.com

Brian Tracey is a business and success trainer with a number of excellent CD 's available His web site is www.briantracey.com

Albert Koopman teaches financial and business development. His material is taught in many universities. His book *"The Quest for The*

Corporate Soul" teaches a better way to run businesses that care about their employees. ISBN 0-9680140-0-3

His web site is albertkoopman1.blogspot.com

BIOGRAPHY

Helen is a senior living in Edmonton, Canada. She began her business life in sales, then as a Realtor specializing in new homes, followed by a stint as a kitchen designer. Finding that she loved management work and helping people she spent over twenty five years in condominium management, ten of those with her own successful business. She contributed many articles on condominium management to the Calgary Herald newspaper and C.C.I. magazine. Helen started her management business in Calgary in 1985. When it was sold ten years later she invested her proceeds in the first of eleven properties. Later selling one a year for tax reasons she began investing in other vehicles, many of high risk. She has been involved in many fields of investing and real estate. Along with her children and grandchildren her greatest loves are learning, sharing her wisdom and developing her spiritual awareness. Her web sites are

www.nanawisewoman.com and www.helenmhamilton.com

Helen M. Hamilton